☙ Very Bad Poetry ❧

Very Bad Poetry

ঙ edited by ও

Kathryn Petras

and

Ross Petras

Vintage Books

A Division of Random House, Inc.

New York

A VINTAGE ORIGINAL, APRIL 1997
First Edition

Library of Congress Cataloging-in-Publication Data
Very bad poetry / edited by Kathryn Petras and
Ross Petras.
p.   cm.
ISBN 0-679-77622-2 (alk. paper)
1. English poetry   2. American poetry.
I. Petras, Kathryn.   II. Petras, Ross.
PR1175.V55   1997
821.008—dc21   96-51788
CIP

Manufactured in the United States of America
10 9 8 7 6 5 4 3 2 1

Fear not, grand eagle
The bay of the beagle!

Fred Emerson Brooks (fl. 1894)
from *"Old Eagle"*

Contents

The Most Convoluted Syntax
On a Procession with the Prince of Wales
by *Joseph Gwyer* 8

Introduction

> *I seemed to feel as it were a strange kind of feeling stealing over me, and remained so for about five minutes. A flame, as Lord Byron has said, seemed to kindle up my entire frame, along with a strong desire to write poetry. . . .*
>
> *It was so strong I imagined that a pen was in my right hand, and a voice crying, "Write Write!" So I said to myself, ruminating, let me see; what shall I write? then all at once a bright idea struck me.*

So did William McGonagall, probably one of the worst poets of the English language, describe his first session with the poetic Muse.

A compulsion to write verse, and a happy delusion regarding talent—that is the beginning of a very bad poet. Very bad poets are perpetrators of a unique and fascinating type of writing. Unlike the plainly bad or the merely mediocre, very bad poetry is powerful stuff. Like great literature, it moves us emotionally, but, of course, it often does so in ways the writer never intended: usually we laugh.

This is no simple task. "Literary is a work very difficult to do," wrote very bad poet Julia Moore in the preface to *A Few Choice Words to the Public.* And she is absolutely correct. To continue her point, very good literary is a work very difficult to do—and so is very bad literary.

Writing very bad poetry requires talent—inverse talent, to be sure, but talent nonetheless. It also helps to have a wooden ear for words, a penchant for sinking into a mire of sentimentality, a bullheaded inclination to stuff too many syllables or words into a line or a phrase, and an enviable confidence that allows one to write despite absolutely appalling incompetence.

Some poets are granted these qualities by the Muse only temporarily—and then they go on to write good poems. Others are blessed, if that is the word, for their entire career.

So what is a very bad poem? Usually it is testimony to a poet's well-honed sense of the anticlimactic. A poet must be immeasurably moved by some grandiose emotion or event—say, a horrific catastrophe—commit it to paper, then veer from the sublime to the pedestrian at precisely the right—which is to say, the wrong—moment. One minute the poet is describing the sinking of a ferry, the next mentioning how much the fare was.

Often it is a matter of using inappropriate words. The poet, eager to keep up a rhyme or meter, shoves in the only word that will do—and, of course, it is the wrong word. ("Fear not, grand eagle, the bay of the beagle" comes to mind.) Or the ever-optimistic poet seems to think that he or she can slip in a word that *almost* rhymes, thus creating exciting and certainly unique not-quite-rhymes such as *Havana* and *manner, pygmies* and *enigmas, mud* and *God*.

And typically very bad poetry bears the weight of over-enthusiastic use of literary devices—alliteration, footnotes, and most commonly, bad metaphors—not to mention bizarre, if excited, imagery, as in the following, by Amanda McKittrick Ros, a bad novelist turned worse poet. (Should the reader wonder, this is a somewhat *different* description of Poets' Corner in Westminster Abbey.)

Holy Moses! Take a look!
Flesh decayed in every nook,
Some rare bits of brain lie here,
Mortal loads of beef and beer.

But ultimately a very bad poem is more than one that violates literary conventions, poetic meter, and grammatical rules. It contains an element of art—that certain something that marks the poem as a masterpiece. As with great art, we can't exactly define a very bad poem except to say we know one when we see one.

And so we are blessed with poems such as "The Spleen," "Ode on the Mammoth Cheese," "A Pindaricque on the Grunting of a Hog," and "An Elegy to a Dissected Puppy." For, as the very bad poet James McIntyre noted, all poets, good and bad,

. . . pursue each theme
Under a gentle head of steam.

This book celebrates these chugging poets.

உ§ Very Bad Poetry ஓ

JOHN ARMSTRONG

(1709–1779)

Not the most compelling personality (a brief biographical entry in a literary encyclopedia includes the following descriptive words: peculiar, melancholic, argumentative, inherent indolence, almost pathological shyness, coarseness, irreverence, bitter, misanthropic, lover of luxury and pomp, querulous), John Armstrong was a Scottish physician who wrote a famous didactic poem on preserving health.

Despite his rather fearsome reputation, a favored few found him "sweet-tempered and whimsical," although those reading "The Art of Preserving Health" might find *bilious* more appropriate.

from The Art of Preserving Health

Book II—Diet

Enough of air. A desert subject now,
Rougher and wilder rises to my sight. . . .

. . .

Half subtilised to chyle, the liquid food
Readiest obeys the assimilating powers;
And soon the tender vegetable mass
Relents. . . .

The languid stomach curses even the pure
Delicious fat, and all the race of oil:
For more, the oily ailments relax
Its feeble tone; and with the eager lymph
(Fond to incorporate all it meets)
Coyly they mix, and shun with slippery wiles

The woo'd embrace. The irresoluble oil,
So gentle late and blandishing, in floods
Of rancid bile o'erflows: what tumults hence,
What horrors rise, were nauseous to relate.
Choose leaner viands, ye whose jovial make
Too fast the gummy nutriment imbibes.

ALFRED AUSTIN

(1835–1913)

In Alfred Austin's monumental *The Human Tragedy*, his heroine, Urania, poses what for the poem is a rather quick question:

> Do you not find Nature's unpunctuality retrieves our
>   too precise
> forebodings, filling up all disappointing vacancies with
>   gifts not
> reckoned in our calendar?

Such is *The Human Tragedy*, which the prolix poet viewed as his magnum opus and over which he labored for many years, through four editions. Although his work was largely ignored by the critics and the public, Austin remained unconcerned, quite convinced of his own Byronic literary genius, which also extended to the writing of plays and an autobiography. According to the latter, his first book bore the wonderful title *Randolph, A Tale of Polish Grief* and sold seventeen copies. Largely because the conservative government wanted a safe, conservative poet, Austin became England's poet laureate.

Supposedly pompous, egotistical, and certainly verbose and prone to using obscure words and phrases, the poet was also known for his breast fixation, which is much in evidence in his poetry. Breasts appear in often unexpected ways or places, often doing unexpected things, such as ploughing the brine or opening doors. A notable specimen of breasts on a platter occurs in Florence:

In that same palace, the Uffizi, I
    Remember to have marked a virgin lift
Upon a silver salver up on high
    The offering of her breasts—no trivial gift.

from *The Human Tragedy*

But the fleet hours pass pitilessly fleeter,
Or where, half-sadly warbling as it went,
Like a boy-poets' happy discontent.

. . .

The stiff wain creaks 'neath the nodding wheat;
    Flit, yaffel, flit from tree to tree.
The babe is hushed on its mother's teat,
And the acorn drops at your dreaming feet,
    Flit, yaffel, flit from tree to tree.
The whimpering winds have lost their way,
    Scream, yaffel, scream from tree to tree.

The following excerpt, from the same extremely long poem, is a
fulmination against what Austin apparently considered a scourge of
mankind—the padded bra.

from *The Human Tragedy*

And do they wear that lubricating lie,
That fleshless falsehood! Palpitating maids
Puff themselves out with hollow buxomness,
To lead some breathless gaby at their heels
A scentless paper chase!

from *"Go Away, Death!"*

Go away, Death!
    You have come too soon.

To sunshine and song I but just awaken,
And the dew on my heart is undried and unshaken;
    Come back at noon.

from *"The Wind Speaks"*

XI

The flocks of the wandering waves I hold
    In the hollows of my hand,
And I let them loose, like a huddled fold,
    And with them I flood the land.

XII

Till they swirl round villages, hamlets, thorpes,
    As the cottagers flee for life:
Then I fling the fisherman's flaccid corpse
    At the feet of the fisherman's wife.

T. BAKER

(fl. 1850s)

Nothing is known of T. Baker, reports D. B. Wyndham Lewis, who rediscovered the poet's work, "except the fact that he was inexhaustibly impressed by the powers of steam"—so much so that Baker wrote a two-hundred-page poem on the steam engine.

from *The Steam Engine*

Canto IV

Lord Stanhope hit upon a novel plan
Of bringing forth this vast Leviathan
(This notion first Genevois' genius struck);
His frame was made to emulate the duck;

Webb'd feet had he, in Ocean's brine to play;
With whale-like might he whirl'd aloft to spray;
But made with all this splash little speed;
Alas! the duck was doom'd not to succeed!

✒ The Most Convoluted Syntax ✒

When in doubt, the very bad poet will commit any syntactical sin imaginable to make a line rhyme—as in the masterpiece excerpted below.

from *On a Procession with the Prince of Wales*

by *Joseph Gwyer*

At evening too the dazzled light
Illumed the darkness of the night
I can't paint it for reasons best.
'Twas grand, though I in crowd was pressed.

SAMUEL BENTLY

(fl. 1760s)

Little is known of Samuel Bently except that he penned the following poem on the death of the Reverend Dean, whose demise one author calls "one of the least moving in literature."

from *The River Dove: A Lyric Pastoral*

Yet here, tho' amusing the Sight,
With Tears the poor Dean* I will mourn;
Who climb'd up this steep, dizzy Height,
By Ways he cou'd never return:
Ah! Why did you ride up so high?
From whence all unheard sing the Birds,
Conduct a Fair Lady: Ah, why!
Where scarce is a Path for the Herds?

How shriek'd the hoarse Ravens a Knell!
When vain, and quite useless the Rein,
All headlong together down fell,
The Horse, the poor Lady, and Dean:
The Lady, by lace-braided Hair
Entangl'd in Brambles was found,
Suspend'd in Brambles was found,
Suspended unhurt in mid-air;
The Dean met his Death with the Ground.

*The Reverend Dean *Langton* and Miss *La Roache,* who were on a visit to Wenman Cokes, Esq., at *Longford,* and went to entertain themselves with a sight of *Dove-dale,* where the Dean was unfortunately killed while attempting to reach the top of one of the rocks, with the lady on the same horse; the lady was saved by the hair of her head being entangled in some bushes.

MRS. MARION ALBINA BIGELOW

(fl. 1850s)

An American poet with a penchant for the melancholy, Mrs. Marion Albina Bigelow was a regular contributor to several periodical columns, turning out poems with bleak titles such as "Two Smothered Children." Of the nearly three hundred poems she wrote, a large number were elegies, often crammed with clinical descriptions of a dying person's last minutes, as in these lines from her poem "Ellen":

> Cold clammy sweats were glistening on her brow;
> Wild with delirium long she struggled there.

Bigelow's depressing outlook (attributed to all her brothers dying from consumption) apparently found an appreciative audience. In fact, the editor of her book of collected poems, *Songs of the St. Lawrence,* found fit to proudly state that "the author is wholly incapable of levity and the reader will find nothing of it in any of her productions."

from *Children Disinterred*

Suggested by seeing four children disinterred,
and placed by the side of their mother

Come, lowly ones, and take your places now
    Beside the mother, who so long had wept,
Had mourn'd your absence with an aching brow,
    And eyes that stream'd with tears while others wept. . . .

. . .

Come, gather round her now! she had not thought
    To see you leave again your mossy tomb—
But ye are rising from that sacred spot;
    The turf is broken—one by one ye come!

Two Smothered Children

Theirs was not the peaceful death-bed,
    Where affection's silent tears,
O'er the couch of pain fast falling,
    Blend with deep responsive prayers;

. . .

Nay, their death was strangely fearful!
    No fond parent closed their eyes,
And no voice of pity answer'd
    To their feebly moaning cries!

E. E. BRADFORD

(1860–1944)

The Reverend Edwin Emanuel Bradford was a prolific writer, churning out about fifteen volumes of verse over the course of twenty-three years. In a zealous, forceful style, he took on topics such as women's rights, which he was apparently against; morality, which he was for; and sin, again against.

This selection, from "The Tree of Knowledge," a longer poem that took on sin, religious belief, and the like, is a cutting indictment of the modern woman.

from *The Tree of Knowledge*

Canto XI *"Equality"*

I

In a sense a bee may be
   Equal to an elephant,
Seeing she can certainly
   Do a score of things he can't:
All the same the fact remains
   She has not his force or brains.

II

That evening when the girls and Ray
Resumed their regulated play,
The lusty lad, more lightly dressed
Rolled up his sleeves and bared his chest,
A sister served: the boy returned.
A ball came bounding back and burned,
As if red-hot, her dainty cheek.
She cried and raved. Ray did not speak,
But let the girls, like angry bees,
Swarm round and sting them at their ease;
And when they all had said their say,
He simply bowed, and strolled away.

III

'I can sting; you can't,'
The bee said, 'and I'll do it.'
She stung the elephant.
He never even knew it!

But soon by chance the burly brute
In passing crushed her with his foot.

His Mother Drinks

Within a London hospital there lies,
　　Tucked in his cot,
A child with golden curls and big blue eyes.
　　The night is hot,
And though the windows in the long low ward
　　Are open wide,
No breath of air comes from the sun-baked yard
　　That lies outside.

. . .

A kindly nurse who sees his wistful smile,
　　To cheer him cries;
"The doctor says that in a little while
　　He'll let you rise,
And send you home again!" His eyes grow dim.
　　She little thinks
What since his father died home means to him—
　　His mother drinks!

✑ The Most Lurid Account of Tragedy ✑

Death, preferably by disaster, is a favorite topic of very bad poets. They eagerly and cheerfully share with their audience every lurid detail. Here is the worst of the worst by one of the most enthusiastic purveyors of what we call "tabloid verse," William McGonagall.

from *Calamity in London;*
Family of Ten Burned to Death
by *William McGonagall*

Oh, Heaven! it was a frightful and pitiful sight to see
Seven bodies charred of the Jarvis family;
And Mrs. Jarvis was found with her child, and both carbonized,
And as the searchers gazed thereon they were surprised.

And these were lying beside the fragments of the bed,
And in a chair the tenth victim was sitting dead;
Oh Horrible! Oh, Horrible! What a sight to behold,
The charred and burnt bodies of both young and old.

COLONEL I. J. BRITTAIN

(fl. 1918)

The colonel was a soldier, a beekeeper, a poet, a publisher, and an entrepreneur from Salem, North Carolina. Although he comes to our attention for his *Brittain's Poems,* which contains his work and that of other poets, he also wrote and published beekeeping guides.

The colonel identifies himself as "an old, disable Confederate Veteran" [sic], but the fact that he survived until 1918 suggests his disability did not affect his general health or his entrepreneurial spirit, which seems quite strong, as evidenced in the following admonition on the cover of his book:

> Never loan this Book to any one. I will keep these Books in stock. Tell them to confine five dimes between two Postal Cards or fifty cents in stamps and this Book will be forthcoming. A Premium with every Book.

from *The Tragedy of Ida Ball Warren
and Samuel Christie*

*This is a true story about the consequences
of an illicit love affair.*

There was a woman lived in Winston-Salem,
  She was beautiful and meek,
She helped to murder her husband,
  Who was found in Muddy Creek.

. . .

He [Christie] conducted with great propriety,
  They thought that he meant no harm,

He went to a neighboring druggist
    And procured chloroform.

They administered it to Warren,
    Put a noose around his neck.
They choked him quite to death.
    As we all do expect.

And when the breath had left him,
    He was nothing but common junk,
    They doubled him up as best they could
    And put him in a trunk.

. . .

He [Christie] took the corpse from the trunk,
    He beat his face to pulp,
Tied weights to his arms and legs,
    And tumbled him into the gulf.

. . .

A fisherman went up the stream,
    He thought he saw a root,
On closer investigation
    He saw it was a human foot.

FRED EMERSON BROOKS

(fl. 1894)

The quintessential multiculturalist, 1890s-style, Fred Emerson Brooks wrote popular collections of popular verse on popular subjects ranging from the bald eagle to babies to battles. He also was extremely partial to that audience-pleasing late-nineteenth-century literary device—writing in dialect. It has been said that audiences attending his poetry readings used to leap to their feet, cheering. And it is no wonder, if one can imagine him reading from a piece such as his "Foreigners on Santa Claus." This multicultural masterpiece gave him a chance to demonstrate his able hand writing in ersatz English, German, Scots, French, Irish, and Italian accents:

> The bonnie Scotchman niver doot
> Wi' Scots Wauhai!
> That Santa Claus goes a' aboot. . . .

segues into

> We have ze Santa Claus een France
> We see him when we get ze chance.

The Stuttering Lover

I lu–love you very well,
Much mu–more than I can tell,
With a lu–lu–lu–lu–love I cannot utter;
I kn–know just what to say
But my tongue gets in the way,
And af–fe–fe–fe–fe–fection's bound to stutter!

When a wooer wu-wu-woos,
And a cooer cu-cu-coos,
Till his face is re-re-red as a tomato,
Take his heart in bi-bi-bits,
Every portion fi-fi-fits,
Though his love song su-su-seem, somewhat staccato!

I'll wu-worship you, of course,
And nu-never get divorce,
Though you stu-stu-stu-stu-storm in angry weather;
For whu-when you're in a pique
So mu-mad you cannot speak,
We'll be du-du-du-du-dumb then both together.

from *Old Eagle*

From thine eyrie, the crag,
Watch over thy flag,
And ne'er let it trail in the dust!
Soaring high in the air
Ever this aegis bear:
"In Freedom and God is our Trust."

Fear not, grand eagle,
The bay of the beagle!

SOLYMAN BROWN

(1790–1876)

Solyman Brown, born in Litchfield, Connecticut, was of that rare breed—poet-dentist. He owned a dental supply store, was a founder of the American Society of Dental Surgeons, and worked with the New York Teeth Manufacturing Company. So it is no wonder his best known literary work is about teeth, the aptly named "Dentologia—A Poem on the Diseases of the Teeth and Their Proper Remedies with Notes, Practical, Historical, Illustrative and Explanatory by Eleazer Parmly, Dentist."

Portions of this poem were published in the *American Journal of Dental Science* and highly praised by its reviewer, who noted that the author not only had a fine grip on the science of dentistry, but also "a mind . . . richly imbued with poetic fancy." The five-canto poem actually helped improve the status of the dental profession. Brown was spurred to write more, turning out next "Dental Hygeia—A Poem," and then, in a startling change of subject, "Cholera King."

from *The Dentologia—A Poem on the Diseases of the Teeth*

. . . her lips disclosed to view,
Those ruined arches, veiled in ebon hue,
Where love had thought to feast the ravished sight
On orient gems reflecting snowy light,
Hope, disappointed, silently retired,
Disgust triumphant came, and love expired!

. . .

Whene'er along the ivory disks, are seen,
The filthy footsteps of the dark gangrene;
When caries come, with stealthy pace to throw

Corrosive ink spots on those banks of snow—
Brook no delay, ye trembling, suffering fair,
But fly for refuge to the dentist's care.

T. E. BROWN

(1830–1897)

A native of the Isle of Man, the Rev. Thomas Edward Brown hoped he could encourage "the great Manx poet" to appear. To this end, he wrote poems not only in English, but also in the Manx dialect. His work had a "peculiar, irresistible flavor," as William Henley, English critic and writer, put it.

Peculiar is the key word here. Brown, who stated that he was "a born sobber," had a tendency to drift a bit into the histrionic and had a singular way of putting things, to say the least. As a *Spectator* review of Brown's poetry said: "We cannot say whether the author of this volume has much gift for poetry of the conventional form. But what he has done he has done well."

Sometimes, however, the unconventional nature of the poetry got just a bit out of hand, as evidenced in the following.

Between Our Folding Lips

Between our folding lips
God slips
An embryon life, and goes;
And this becomes your rose.
We love, God makes: in our sweet mirth

God spies occasion for a birth.
Then is it his, or is it ours?
I know not—He is fond of flowers.

WALLACE BRUCE

(fl. 1907)

An American poet who flourished in the early 1900s, Wallace Bruce published at least six books of verse in handsome gilt-covered editions. Bruce garnered a fair amount of praise from readers and critics alike. The *Times* said his poems were "sprightly and graceful." John Greenleaf Whittier found them "fine and fitting." The poet was fond of bucolic, historic, and occasionally lighter themes. To our knowledge he is the only poet to have found inspiration in a brick.

A Holland Brick

O Jolly brick, with kindly wrinkled face,
    With ruddy cheek and hospitable look,
By Knickerbocker you shall have a place
    And on my mantel stand, my quaintest book.

Epitome of hearty, happy days,
    When even bricks were honest, good and true;
A gentle humor o'er your visage plays—
    With heart and hand I welcome you.

H. C. BUNNER

(FL. 1880s)

New Yorker H. C. Bunner was the editor of *Puck* magazine and a writer of novels and poetry. Although *Nation* magazine termed his first book of poetry, *Airs from Araby,* "a rather commonplace volume," the collection contains poems that aren't all that commonplace. Instead, it seems that Bunner periodically took the name of his magazine a little too much to heart . . . and was a bit more puckish than perhaps he should have been.

from *In School House*

A Real Romance

The boy with a fair-curled head
    Smiles with masculine scorn,
When the sad small note is read,
    With its straggling script forlorn:
"Charley, wy is it you won't
    Forgive me laughing at you?
I will kill my self if you don't
    Honest I will for true!"

. . .

To the teacher's ears like a dream
    The school-room noises float—
Then a sudden bustle—a scream
    From a girl—"She has cut her throat!"
And the poor little hunchbacked chap
    From his corner leaps like a flash—
Has her death-like head in his lap—
    And his fingers upon the gash.

'T is not deep. An "eraser" blade
>Was the chosen weapon of death;
And the face on the boy's knee laid
>Is alive with a fluttering breath.
But faint from the shock and fright,
>She lies, too weak to be stirred,
Blood-stained, inky and white,
>Pathetic, small, absurd.

The cruel Adonis stands
>Much scared and woe-begone now;
Smoothing with nervous hands
>The damp hair off her brow.
He is penitent, through and through;
>And she—she is satisfied.
Knowing my sex as I do,
>I wish I could add: She died.

from *Their Wedding Journey*

Dear Mother,
>When the coach rolled off
>From dear old Battery Place,
I hid my face within my hands—
>That is, I hid my face.

J. GORDON COOGLER

(1865–1901)

"Poems Written While You Wait" was the sign on J. Gordon Coogler's print shop in Charleston, South Carolina. This prolific author of "Purely Original Verse" enjoyed an ambiguous popularity in his brief career as a poet, selling thousands of copies of his first two books, and living to see many fan clubs formed. In many cases his following was not so much due to the merits of his poetry but rather the reverse.

Reviews of his poetry may be politely termed "mixed," but that would be stretching the truth. "Wretched taste," said *Puck* in 1894; on the other hand, the *Atlanta Constitution* said that "there must be something in the writings of a man who can attract attention and win applause when corn is thirty cents a bushel and potato bugs have become a burden."

Coogler seemed blissfully convinced of his own brilliance. A Methodist Sunday school teacher who often wrote of "the gentler sex and their temptations," Coogler was a straitlaced gentleman of the old school. As he put it: "You'll never see this form clad in gaudy apparel, nor these feet playing the 'dude' in patent leather shoes."

Alas Carolina

Alas! Carolina! Carolina! Fair land of my birth,
    Thy fame will be wafted from the mountain to the sea
As being the greatest educational centre on earth.
    At the cost of men's blood thro' thy "one X" whiskey.

Two very large elephants* thou has lately installed,
    Where thy sons and daughters are invited to come,
And learn to be physically fit and mentally strong,
    By the solemn proceeds of thy "innocent rum."

*Winthrop and Clemson colleges.

Here Coogler puts his own modern twist on the damsel in distress theme. A pretty woman of "dove-like form" is about to fall from her bicycle.

from *The Lover's Return on a Bicycle*
Admitted, but not accepted

Her charming steel-horse could not miss
A steep and dangerous precipice
      By the river's bank;
Along she flew—a fearful sight—
Like a bird wounded in its flight
      She downward sank

Many an anxious eye drew near,
And gazing with a sense of fear,
      Looked here and there;
No wounded form could there be found,
Nor trace of blood seen on the ground,
      Of the maiden fair.

For safe below the rough incline
She passed beneath the Southern pine—
      Her charming wheel
Never faltering, stood it all,
Thus saving her from a fatal fall
      By its perfect steel.

[*Untitled*]

O that the lilies and roses were mine
Instead of the oak and ivy of life.

from *How Strange Are Dreams!*

How strange are dreams! I dreamed the other night
    A dream that made me tremble,
        Not with fear, but with a kind of strange reality;
My supper, though late, consisted of no cheese.

Coogler's enigmatic hatred of Byron's mother was noted by contemporaries, who, like us, have no explanations.

Byron

Oh, thou immortal bard!
Men may condemn the song
    That issued from thy heart sublime,
Yet alas! its music sweet
Has left an echo that will sound
    Thro' the lone corridors of Time.

Thou immortal Byron!
Thy inspired genius
    Let no man attempt to smother—
May all that was good within thee
Be attributed to Heaven,
    All that was evil—to thy mother.

A Pretty Girl

On her beautiful face there are smiles of grace
    That linger in beauty serene,
And there are no pimples encircling her dimples,
    As ever, as yet, I have seen.

More Care for the Neck Than for the Intellect

Fair lady, on that snowy neck and half-clad bosom
Which you so publicly reveal to man,
    There's not a single outward stain or speck;
Would that you had given but half the care
To the training of your intellect and heart
    As you have given to that spotless neck.

For Time, alas! must touch with cold unerring hand,
That fair bosom's soft, untarnished hue,
    Staining that lily-leaf of your sweet sex;
Then in ignorance you will journey here below,
Hiding that once fair bosom 'neath a veil,
    With a standing collar 'round your wrinkled neck.

God Correctly Understood

The man who thinks God is too kind
To punish actions vile,
Is bad at heart, of unsound mind
Or very juvenile.

❧ The Poem Showing the Most ❧ Mathematical Genius

Little is known of the poet who wrote the following, Frederick B. Needham, except that he lived in the mid-1800s—and, as the following lines show, that he could count.

from *The Round of the Clock*
by Frederick B. Needham

"One!" strikes the clock in the belfry tower,
Which but sixty minutes ago
Sounded twelve for the midnight hour.

ELIZA COOK

(1818–1889)

Eliza Cook burst onto the literary scene with her poem "I'm Afloat!" A succession of verse works followed. Later the successful poet was even asked to edit her own periodical: *Eliza Cook's Journal*. Her middle-class public adored her, and critics praised her "sympathy with all that is good and true."

The poet's truth-telling Muse extended to topics such as household furniture. Her poem "The Old Armchair" was one of her most beloved poems. It included the opening lines

> I love it, I love it; and who shall dare
> To chide me for loving that old Arm-chair?

But usually Cook concentrated on naturalistic and heroic themes, sometimes with a touch of the macabre. Her book *Melaia, and Other Poems* went into three editions and was also published in New York. Its title poem, about the loyalty of a dog to its master, spawned a hot literary debate: was the dog a retriever or another breed?

Cook had a strong Victorian sense of mission. "I am anxious," she once said, "to give my feeble aid to the titanic struggle for intellectual elevation now going on."

from *The Surgeon's Knife*

There are hearts—stout hearts,—that own no fear
At the whirling sword or the darting spear,—
that are ready alike to bleed in the dust,
'Neath the sabre's cut or the bayonet's thrust;
They heed not the blows that Fate may deal,
From the murderer's dirk or the soldier's steel:
But lips that laugh at the dagger of strife
Turn silent and white from the surgeon's knife.

. . . It shines in the grasp—'tis no weapon for play,
A shudder betrays it is speeding its way;
While the quivering muscle and severing joint
Are gashed by the keen edge and probed by the point.
. . . Dripping it comes from the cells of life,
While glazing eyes turn from the surgeon's knife.

Here the author takes us inside the mind of a crow that feeds on
dead humans.

from *The Carrion Crow*

I plunged my beak in the marbling cheek,
I perched on the clammy brow:
And a dainty treat was that fresh meat
To the greedy Carrion Crow.

. . .

And quickly his breast had a table guest,
In the hungry Carrion Crow.

from *Lines Among the Leaves*

A varied theme it utters,
Where the glossy date-leaf flutters;
A loud and lightsome chant it yieldeth there;
And the quiet, listening dreamer,
May believe that many a streamer
        Flaps the air.

It is sad and dreary hearing
Where the giant pine is rearing
A lone head, like a hearse plume waved about;
And it lurketh melancholy
where the thick and somber holly
Bristles out.

The following passage from a longer poem concerns the horrible
trials of a ship becalmed in the tropics.

from *Song of the Sea Weed*

Many a lip is gaping for drink,
And madly calling for rain;
And some hot brains are beginning to think
Of a messmate's opened vein.

A Pathetic Lament

*(On people visiting a castle to find its owner away and no
food set out for visitors)*

The castle was nigh, with its towers so high
And the flag mast poking its nose to the sky;
The walls were as grey as the farewell of day,
When the muffin-boy goes on his wandering way.

The ivy was green in the Midsummer sheen,
With as noble a watch dog as ever was seen;

All things were enriching the prospect bewitching
Expecting a little black smoke from the kitchen.

We had conjured up dreams of rare Burgundy streams,
Of terrestrial cake and ethereal creams;
With the zeal of a Milton our fancies had built on
The hopes of some precious old port with ripe Stilton.

The soul-stirring line may be all very fine,
Provided the minstrel can manage to dine;
But to stand 'neath a portal where the commons are short
    all,
Takes a great deal of sentiment out of the mortal.

We sat in despair, with a starvation stare,—
Not a plate, not a dish, not a cover was there;
Not the chink of a fork nor the creak of a cork,
To announce that the butler was doing his work.

LILLIAN E. CURTIS

(fl. 1870s)

Lillian Curtis was a native of Chicago best known for writing sentimental verse on the banal, the bathetic, and, often, the bleak. Her first book, *Forget-Me-Not,* published in 1872, contained such uplifting and educational poems as "We All Must Pass Away" and "An Inventory," which itemizes the contents of "a drunkard's hut," complete with the sorry hut owner himself, described as "a haggard man . . . uttering wild and piercing cries."

Forget-Me-Not "paved the way to a castle of literary hopes for the future," as Curtis wrote in the introduction to her second book, *Patchwork.* She explained that she had actually intended to publish another book, *The Casket,* but since the manuscript was destroyed in the fire of July 14, 1874, she hastily cobbled together "a patched-up substitute." Ever the moralizer, Curtis closed by pointing out that had it not been for the fire, *Patchwork* would never have been published, "but, alas, on just such slender threads hang even the greatest of life's events."

Only One Eye

Oh! she was a lovely girl,
　　So pretty and so fair,
With gentle, lovelit eyes,
　　And wavy, dark-brown hair.

I loved the gentle girl,
　　But oh! I heaved a sigh,
When first she told me she could see
　　Out of only one eye.

But soon I thought within myself,
　　I'd better save my tear and sigh,
To bestow upon some I know,
　　Who has *more* than one eye.

She is brave and intelligent,
　　Too she is witty and wise,
She'll accomplish more now, than many,
　　Who have two eyes.

Ah! you need not pity her,
　　She needs not your tear and sigh,
She makes good use, I tell you,
　　Of her one remaining eye.

In the home where we are hastening,
    In our eternal Home on High,
See that you be not rivaled,
    By the girl with only *one* eye.

The Potato

What on this wide earth,
    That is made, or does by nature grow,
Is more homely, yet more beautiful,
    Than the useful Potato?

What would this world full of people do,
    Rich and poor, high and low,
Were it not for this little-thought-of
    But very necessary Potato?

True 'tis homely to look on,
    Nothing pretty in even its blow,
But it will bear acquaintance,
    This useful Potato.

For when it is cooked and opened,
    It's so white and mellow,
You forget it ever was homely,
    This useful Potato.

On the whole it is a very plain plant,
    Makes no conspicuous show.
But the internal appearance is lovely,
    Of the unostentatious Potato.

The useful and the beautiful
    Are not far apart we know.
And thus the beautiful are glad to have,
    The homely looking Potato.

On the land, or on the sea,
    Wherever we may go,
We are always glad to welcome
    The homely Potato.

A practical and moral lesson
    This may plainly show,
That though homely, our heart *can be*
    Like that of the homely Potato.

The Two Bears

There are two bears that near us we should allow to dwell,
Nor e'er by harsh word or hasty act can repel,
Homes and lives can only be happy made,
    Where these two bears are allowed to stay,
And the foundation for enjoyment is laid,
    Where these two bears haunt the way.
Oh, send them never crossly from the door,
But let them remain one's sight before,
For they'll ne'er bring grief nor sorrow,
    Nor ever a thought of pending sadness,
They'll point out many a bright tomorrow,
    And fill it with joy and gladness.
Those two bears we should nourish e'er with care,
Their names, remember, are Bear and Forbear.

J. P. DUNN

(fl. 1917)

J. P. Dunn, or "J. P. Dunn, Author," as he styles himself on his book of poems, was a loyal Kansan who evidently sought to combine poetry with pesticide application. As such, in his only book extant, rather appropriately titled *The Plains: Poems in Kansas and Agriculture, Plant, Prune and Spray,* poems give way to terse prose on cankerworm and tent caterpillars. Dunn's other main concern is to work into his poetry as many Kansas counties, persons, or landmarks as euphonically possible.

Dunn's reputation among his contemporaries is unknown, but he reports that his poems had been published in many newspapers, including the St. Louis *Globe Democrat* and Ottawa *Herald,* and the Capper's *Weekly.*

In the following work the poet meets a challenge—working in county names in a paean to his home state.

Kansas

It is springtime out here in Kansas;
Many eagles now are seen
Flying over the hills and rivers,
Of the Smoky and Saline.

. . .

The antelope and buffalo,
The broad horned elk and deer
Are extinct from the Smoky hills
But on the western slope are seen
The prairie dogs and gophers

Still playfully bark and play,
In the counties of McPherson,
Lincoln, Saline, and Clay.

An Ode to Governor Capper

The sun rises in the ancient east,
But sets in Kansas' modern west,
Where all men and women are equal
And everything is the very best. . . .

. . .

We are blest out here in Kansas,
With sunshine, air and rain. . . .
Our women are most beautiful,
All can bake, wash and iron,
And our virgins true to their sweethearts,
And sure to treat the husbands fi-ine. . . .

. . .

I will quote words from Governor Capper
From a speech he made last fall
That Kansas can raise grain enough
To feed all our allies that are now engaged in war.
We believe it because he said it.
And with Western pride affirm,
That whatever Governor Capper says,
You can rely upon.

EDWARD EDWIN FOOT

(fl. 1867)

Edward Edwin Foot, by fortunate accident of birth, was aptly named: he was an avid footnoter. Readers of his poetry never have to struggle for a meaning; Foot makes everything perfectly clear by appending footnotes whenever he feels it is necessary (which is often). He wrote only one book of poetry, *The Original Poems of Edward Edwin Foot of Her Majesty's Customs*—possibly the only poetry book that came with the recommendation of Sir F. H. Doyle, Bart., Receiver-General of H.M. Customs, and probably the only poetry book containing footnotes longer than the actual lines of verse.

from *Jane Hollybrand; or, Virtue Rewarded*

Lord Arnold delicately sought to name
The nuptial-day, and urg'd the blushing Jane
To fix the date; but she with subdued voice,
Begg'd courteously to be excused,—'the choice,'
She softly said, 'dear Arnold' should be thine;
And what your wish may be, that shall be mine.'
He then, most fondly, kiss'd her modest cheek,
And named it for the following Wednesday week:
'Shall it be so?' he said . . .'Come, dear, express
Thy pleasure and enhance my happiness!'
She press'd his hand, and breathed the mono-word[1]
To which George Hollybrand at once concurr'd.

1. 'Yes!'

from *The Homeward-Bound Passenger Ship*

The captain scans the ruffled zone,[1]
    And heeds the wind's increasing scope;
He knows full well, and reckons on
    His seamanship, but God's his hope. . . .

Look, look ye down the plumbless deep,
    See,[2] if ye can, their lifeless forms!—
Here laid, poor things! across a steep,
    An infant in its mother's arms.

1. A figurative expression, intended by the Author to signify the horizon.

2. Imagine.

The following selection deserves special notice for the ratio of poem text to footnote text. It's also notable because despite the footnotes the meaning of the poem is still unclear.

[*Untitled*]

Altho' we[1] mourn for one now gone,
And he—that grey-hair'd Palmerston,[2]
    We will give God the praise,—
For he, beyond the age of man,[3]
Eleven years had over-ran
    Within two equal days.

1. The nation.

2. The Right Honourable Henry John Temple, Viscount Palmerston, K.G., G.C.B., etc. (the then Premier of the British Government), died at "Brockett Hall," Herts., at a quarter to eleven o'clock in the forenoon of Wednesday, 18th October, 1865, aged eighty-one years (all but two days), having been born on the 20th October, 1784. The above lines were written on the occasion of his death.

3. Scriptural limitation.

❧ The Worst Baby Talk Poem ❧

A particularly nauseating subset of very bad poetry centers on baby talk, and baby's view of the world—"so-o big"—and baby—"so-o 'ittle."

This is the worst baby talk poem ever written—one that, to paraphrase Dorothy Parker, might make you fwow up.

The New Baby

by Fred Emerson Brooks

Tind friends, I pray extuse me
　　From matin' any speech,
Betause I is so 'ittle
　　I ain't dot much for each;
There ain't much edutation
　　In such a 'ittle head;
Besides, I is so s'eepy
　　An' wants to do to bed. . . .

. . .

She's found anuzzer baby
　　Dat's noisier than I,
Betause it don't do noffin'
　　But stay in bed an' cwy.
She found it in the garret;
　　I dess it's dumb an' deef;
It's such a funny toler,
　　An' ain't dot any teef;
An' aint dot any eyebrows,
　　An' ain't dot any hair;
In fact, it ain't dot noffin,
　　Nor any shoes to wear.

SAM WALTER FOSS

(1858–1911)

S. W. Foss was a graduate of Brown University in Providence, Rhode Island, and later editor of the Boston *Yankee Blade*. He submitted and sold many poems to Northeastern newspapers—mostly light, didactic verse in a get-up-and-go Babbitt style.

"Hullo!"

W'en you see a man in woe,
Walk right up an' say, "Hullo!"
Say "Hullo!" an' "How d'ye do?"
"How's the world a-usin' you?"
Slap the fellow on his back;
Bring your han' down with a whack!
Waltz right up, an' don't go slow;
Grin an' shake an' say "Hullo!"

Is he clothed in rags? Oh, sho!
Walk right up an' say, "Hullo!"
Rags is but a cotton roll
Jest for wrappin' up a soul;
An' a soul is worth a true
Hale an' hearty "How d'ye do?"
Don't wait for the crowd to go;
Walk right up an' say "Hullo!"

W'en big vessels meet, they say,
They saloot an' sail away.
Jest the same are you an' me—
Lonesome ships upon a sea;

Each one sailin' his own jog
For a port beyond the fog.
Let yer speakin' trumpet blow,
Lift yer horn an' cry "Hullo!"

Say "Hullo!" an' "How d'ye do?"
Other folks are good as you.
W'en ye leave yer house of clay,
Wanderin' in the Far-Away;
W'en you travel through the strange
Country t'other side the range;
Then the souls you've cheered will know
Who ye be, an' say "Hullo!"

JAMES GRAINGER

(1721–1767)

James Grainger called himself "a ruptured poet lost in holy trance." The meaning of this expression is uncertain, but, then, Grainger had rather an unorthodox way of putting things. He is best known for his long, dense, information-rich poem about sugarcane, or, more specifically, how to grow the crop in the West Indies, a work titled simply "The Sugar Cane."

Upon hearing about Grainger's intentions, Dr. Samuel Johnson had perhaps the logical reaction: "What could Grainger make of a sugar-cane? One might as well write "The Parsley Bed—A Poem,"" or, "The Cabbage Garden—A Poem." Happily for us, Grainger ignored the criticism and went ahead with his botanic masterpiece.

Unfortunately, one of Grainger's worst lines of poetry—and possibly one of the worst *ever* written—was cut from the poem. According to Boswell's *Life of Johnson,* Grainger read the manuscript to a group of friends at the home of Sir Joshua Reynolds:

. . . all the assembled wits burst into a laugh when, after much blank verse pomp, the poet began a new paragraph thus:

> 'Now, Muse, let's sing of *rats.*'

And what increased the ridicule was, that one of the company who slyly overlooked the reader, perceived that the word had been originally *mice,* and had been altered to *rats,* as more dignified.

A different version of the events was told by Miss Reynolds. According to her, Grainger had reached the line "Say, shall I sing of rats?" at which point Dr. Johnson yelled out "No!" Whichever version is correct, the provocative line was changed—but fortunately, the poem lost none of its unique qualities.

from *The Sugar Cane*

Of composts shall the Muse disdain to sing?
Nor soil her heavenly plumes? The sacred Muse
Nought sordid deems, but what is base; nought fair,
Unless true Virtue stamp it with her seal.
Then, planter, wouldst thou double thine estate,
Never, ah! never, be asham'd to tread
Thy dung heaps.

Whether the fattening compost in each hole
'Tis best to throw; or, on the surface spread;
Is undetermin'd: Trials must decide.
Unless kind rains and fostering dews descend,
To melt the compost's fertilizing salts;
A stinted plant, deceitful of thy hopes,
Will from those beds slow spring where hot dung lies:

But, if 'tis scatter'd generously o'er all,
The Cane will better bear the solar blaze;
Less rain demand; and, by repeated crops,
Thy land improv'd, its gratitude will show.
Enough of composts, Muse; of soils, enough:
When best to dig, and when inhume the Cane;
A task how arduous! next demands thy song.

Another example of Grainger's poetry, this selection, like "The Sugar Cane" is set in the West Indies, Grainger's adopted home, but is much less pedantic and much more romantic . . . if a bit gory.

from *Bryan and Pereene*

A West Indian Ballad

The north-east wind did briskly blow,
　　The ship was safely moor'd,
Young Bryan thought the boat's crew slow,
　　And so leapt overboard.

Pereene, the pride of Indian dames,
　　His heart did long enthrall,
And whoso his impatience blames,
　　I wot, ne'er lov'd at all.

. . .

In sea-green silk so neatly clad,
　　She there impatient stood;
The crew with wonder saw the lad
　　Repel the foaming flood.

Her hands a handkerchief display'd,
    Which he at parting gave;
Well pleas'd, the token he survey'd
    And manlier beat the wave.

Her fair companions, one and all,
    Rejoicing crowd the strand;
For now her lover swam in call,
    And almost touch'd the land.

Then through the white surf did she haste,
    To clasp her lovely swain;
When, ah! a shark bit through his waist:
    His heart's bloody'd the main!

He shriek'd his half sprung from the wave,
    Streaming with purple gore,
And soon it found a living grave,
    And, ah! was seen no more.

MATTHEW GREEN

(1697–1737)

A poet and customs officer (like Edwin Edward Foot after him), Matthew Green was considered a wit. Perhaps it was his quick thinking that led him to write one of his most famous poems, about the often-overlooked spleen. "The Spleen" was quite successful. It was published posthumously in 1737 by Richard Glover, author of the epic *Leonidas,* and subsequently appeared in the famous *Dodsley's Collection,* as well as in Dr. Johnson's *Poets.* And none other than the poet laureate Alexander Pope said that there was a great deal of originality in the poem—a sentiment with which few can argue.

from *The Spleen*

I always choose the plainest food
To mend viscidity of blood.
Hail! water gruel, healing power,
Of easy access to the poor;
Thy help love's confessors implore,
And doctors secretly adore:
To thee I fly, by thee dilute—
Through veins my blood doth quicker shoot;
And by swift current throws off clean
Prolific particles of spleen.

JOSEPH GWYER

(1835-?)

Joseph Gwyer was a potato salesman with a dream: to be poet laureate of England. So he devoted those hours when he wasn't selling potatoes to this estimable end. For twenty years he wrote furiously, sending his works to Buckingham Palace and getting time after time the royal equivalents of a rejection letter—curt acknowledgments from private secretaries. But the ever-optimistic Gwyer read these as recommendations. In 1875 he published a collection of his works: *Sketches of the Life of Joseph Gwyer (Potato Salesman) with His Poems (Commended by Royalty)* and included reprints of some of the letters he had received as well as some reviews he had collected—which were about as evasive as the royal letters; for instance, "Mr. Gwyer's aspirations are most praiseworthy. . . . we prefer to refrain from depreciating that which is so well intentioned," read a review in *Lloyd's Weekly*.

Always the salesman, Gwyer also presented readers of the book with a unique opportunity: people could purchase by mail a sack of his potatoes as well, not to mention a photograph of him and his horse. A review of the book in the *New York Tribune* was blunt: people who weren't sure whether to opt for the poetry or the potatoes should choose the potatoes.

To Alfred Gwyer

I wish you Alfred now a good night;
You gives your mother great delight;
Don't you wake up and ask for baa,
Or you'll offend your dad-dad-a.

(Note: Alfred, when asking for bread, calls it baa; and water, waa.)

from *Ode on the Visit of the Shah of Persia*

Intoxicating draughts he never does drink
If this we copied should we not be better, think?

from *On the Death of the Duke of Clarence*

Albert Victor loved his mother,
Father, sisters and his brother,
Affection great marked here his stay,
Was kind disposed in every way.

from *On the Funeral of Dr. Livingston*

Heap on more grass was his request
As hapless now he laid to rest.

NANCY LUCE

(fl. 1860s)

Nancy Luce lived on a farm in Martha's Vineyard, was certainly
fond of chickens, and published a book of verse and advice called
Poor Little Hearts.

This selection was sent to us by the distinguished modern poet
W. D. Snodgrass, who, with his wife, does a reading of bad verse
called "The Murdered Muse."

from *Poor Little Hearts*

*Lines composed by Nancy Luce about poor little Ada Queetie,
and poor little Beauty Linna, both deceased. Poor little Ada
Queetie died February 25th, Thursday night, at 12 o'clock,
aged most 9 years. Poor little Beauty Linna died January 18th,
Tuesday night, most 2 o'clock, 1859, aged over 12 years. She
lived 11 months lacking 7 days after poor sissy's decease.*

Poor little Ada Queetie has departed this life,
Never to be here no more,
No more to love, no more to speak.

. . .

Poor little Ada Queetie's last sickness and death,
Destroyed my health at an unknown rate,
With my heart breaking and weeping,
I kept the fire going night after night, to keep poor little
    dear warm,
Poor little heart, she was sick one week
With froth in her throat,
Then 10 days and grew worse, with dropsy in her stomach,
I kept getting up nights to see how she was.

. . .

She was coming 9 years of age, when she was taken away,
By all I found out, very certain true
Poor Sissy hatched her out her egg in Chilmark,
The reason she was taken away before poor Sissy,
Her constitution was as weak as weak could be.

. . .

She would do 34 wonderful cunning things,
Poor Sissy would do 39,
They would do part of them without telling,
And do all the rest with telling.

. . .

When she used to be in her little box to lay pretty egg,
She would peek up from under the chair.

. . .

Her complaint that caused her death,
Was just such a complaint as poor Sissy had
Only poor Sissy's complaint ended with dropsy in her
    stomach.

WILLIAM MCGONAGALL

(1830–1902)

As William McGonagall, self-described poet and tragedian, wrote in the opening to his *Poetic Gems,* "The most startling incident in my life was the time I discovered myself to be a poet."

Many people in his native Dundee, Scotland, apparently disagreed with his discovery. Once while he was reciting his work at a pub, a waiter threw a wet towel at him. Yet McGonagall tried to put a positive spin on events. As McGonagall tells it, "While . . . giving a good recitation, it helps to arrest the company's attention from the drink. . . . Such was the case with me." So the pub owner, upset that everyone was listening to McGonagall and not drinking up, had the waiter throw the towel at McGonagall and so end the poetry reading.

Another time a publican threw peas at McGonagall. Once again the poet had a positive interpretation. "The reason, I think for the publican throwing peas at me," he wrote in a preface, "is because I say, to the devil with your glass in my song, 'The Rattling Boy from Dublin,' and he, no doubt considered it had a teetotal tendency about it, and, for that reason, he had felt angry, and had thrown the peas at me."

McGonagall was what is politely termed a "naive" poet. In other words, he had no ear for meter, a knack for choosing the most banal of subjects, and a tendency to stretch mightily for a rhyme. But the overall effect was uniformly entertaining. He drew great crowds to his readings, in spite of—or, more accurately, because of—his lack of talent.

The following three selections concerning a railway bridge built over Dundee's river Tay are best read in swift succession.

from *The Railway Bridge of the Silvery Tay*

Beautiful Railway Bridge of the Silvery Tay!
With your numerous arches and pillars in so grand array,
And your central girders, which seem to the eye
To be almost towering to the sky.
The greatest wonder of the day,
And a great beautification to the River Tay,
Most beautiful to be seen,
Near by Dundee and the Magdalen Green.

Beautiful Railway Bridge of the Silvery Tay!
That has caused the Emperor of Brazil to leave
His home far away, incognito in his dress,
And view thee ere he passed along en route to Inverness.

. . .

Beautiful Railway Bridge of the Silvery Tay!
I hope that God will protect all passengers
By night and by day,
And that no accident will befall them while crossing
The Bridge of the Silvery Tay,
For that would be most awful to be seen
Near by Dundee and the Magdalen Green.

The Tay Bridge Disaster

Beautiful Railway Bridge of the Silv'ry Tay
Alas! I am very sorry to say
That ninety lives have been taken away
On the last Sabbath day of 1879,
Which will be remembered for a very long time.

'Twas about seven o'clock at night,
And the wind it blew with all its might,
And the rain came pouring down,
And the dark clouds seem'd to frown,
And the Demon of the air seem'd to say—
"I'll blow down the Bridge of Tay."

. . .

It must have been an awful sight,
To witness in the dusky moonlight,
While the Storm Fiend did laugh, and angry did bray,
Along the Railway Bridge of the Silv'ry Tay.
Oh! ill-fated Bridge of the Sil'vry Tay,
I must now conclude my lay
By telling the world fearlessly without the least dismay,
That your central girders would not have given way,
At least many sensible men do say,
Had they been supported on each side with buttresses,
At least many sensible men confesses,
For the stronger we our houses do build,
The less chance we have of being killed.

from *An Address to the New Tay Bridge*

Beautiful new railway bridge of the Silvery Tay,
With your strong brick piers and buttresses in so grand array,
And your thirteen central girders, which seem to my eye
Strong enough all windy storms to defy.

from *A Tale of the Sea*

'Twas on the 8th April, on the afternoon of that day,
That the little village of Louisberg was thrown into a wild
    state of dismay,
And the villagers flew to the beach in a state of wild uproar,
And in a dory they found four men were cast ashore.

Then the villagers, in surprise, assembled about the dory,
And they found that the bottom of the boat was gory;
Then their hearts were seized with sudden dread,
When they discovered that two of the men were dead.

And the two survivors were exhausted from exposure,
    hunger, and cold,
Which caused the spectators to shudder when them they
    did behold. . . .

They were carried to a boarding-house without delay,
But those that were looking on were stricken with dismay,
When the remains of James and Angus M'Donald were
    found in the boat,
Likewise three pieces of flesh in a pool of blood afloat.

Angus M'Donald's right arm was missing from the elbow,
And the throat was cut in a sickening manner, which filled
    the villagers' hearts with woe,
Especially when they say two pieces of flesh had been cut
    from each thigh,
'Twas then the kind-hearted villagers did murmur and sigh.

Here is McGonagall at his name-dropping best—careful to include virtually every mourner and/or floral tribute.

from *The Death of Lord and Lady Dalhousie*

Alas! Lord and Lady Dalhousie are dead, and buried at last,
Which causes many people to feel a little downcast;
And both lie side by side in one grave,
But I hope God in His goodness their souls will save.

. . .

'Twas in the year of 1887, and on Thursday the 1st of
   December,
Which his relatives and friend will long remember
That were present at the funeral in Cockpen churchyard,
Because they had for the noble Lord a great regard.

About eleven o'clock the remains reached Dalhousie,
And were met by a body of the tenantry;
They conveyed them inside the building, all seemingly
   woebegone,
And among those that sent wreaths was Lord Claude
   Hamilton.

Those that sent wreaths were but very few,
But one in particular was the Duke of Bucceleuch
Besides Dr. Herbert Spencer, and Countess Rosebery, and
   Lady Bennett,
Which no doubt were sent by them with heartfelt regret.

Besides those that sent wreaths in addition were the Earl
   and Countess of Aberdeen,
Especially the Prince of Wales' was most lovely to be seen,

And the Earl of Dalkeith's wreath was very pretty too,
With a mixture of green and white flowers, beautiful to view.

Amongst those present at the interment were Mr. Marjoribanks, M.P.,
Also ex-Provost Ballingall from Bonnie Dundee;
Besides the Honourable W. G. Colville, representing the Duke and Duchess of Edinburgh,
While in everyone's face standing at the grave was depicted sorrow.

Another of McGonagall's pieces marking a historic event, "The Funeral of the German Emperor," is also a wonderful example of the poet's penchant for banal descriptions.

from *The Funeral of the German Emperor*

As the procession passes the palace the blinds are drawn completely,
And every house is half hidden with the sable drapery;
And along the line of march expansive arches were erected,
While the spectators standing by seemed very dejected.

. . .

The whole distance to the grave was covered over with laurel and bay,
So that the body should be borne along smoothly all the way;
And the thousands of banners in the processions were beautiful to view,

Because they were composed of cream-coloured silk and
   light blue.

The poet here celebrates the harpooning of the Tay whale, which
was then towed into port.

from *The Famous Tay Whale*

And my opinion is that God sent the whale in time of
   need,
No matter what other people may think or what is their
   creed;
I know fishermen in general are often very poor,
And God in his goodness sent it to drive poverty from
   their door.

So Mr. John Wood has bought it for two hundred and
   twenty-six pound,
And has brought it to Dundee all safe and all sound;
Which measures 40 feet in length from the snout to the
   tail,
So I advise the people far and near to see it without fail.

Then hurrah! for the mighty monster whale,
Which has got 17 feet 4 inches from tip to tip of a tail!
Which can be seen for a sixpence of a shilling,
That is to say, if the people are all willing.

The Late Sir John Ogilvy

Alas! Sir John Ogilvy is dead, aged eighty-seven,
But I hope his soul is now in heaven;
For he was a generous-hearted gentleman I am sure,
And, in particular, very kind unto the poor.

. . .

He was a public benefactor in many ways,
Especially in erecting an asylum for imbecile children to
    spend their days;
Then he handed the institution over as free,—
As a free gift and a boon to the people of Dundee.

from *The Royal Review*
August 25, 1881

All hail to the Empress of India, Great Britain's Queen—
Long may she live in health, happy and serene—
That came from London, far away,
To review the Scottish Volunteers in grand array:
Most magnificent to be seen,
Near by Salisbury Crags and its pastures green,
Which will long be remembered by our gracious Queen—

And by the Volunteers, that came from far away,
Because it rain'd most of the day.
And with the rain their clothes were wet all through,
On the 25th day of August, at the Royal Review.
And to the Volunteers it was no lark,
Because they were ankle deep in mud in the Queen's Park.

The following poem is, to our knowledge, the only one ever written about Alois Senefelder.

from *The Sprig of Moss*

[B]y taking the impressions of watch-cases he discovered, one day
What is now called the art of Lithography.
So Alois plodded on making known his great discovery,
Until he obtained the notice of the Royal Academy,
Besides, he obtained a gold Medal, and what was more dear to his heart,
He lived to see the wide extension of his art.

And when life's prospects may at times appear dreary to ye,
Remember Alois Senefelder, the discoverer of Lithography.

from *The Clepington Catastrophe*

Accidents will happen by land and by sea,
Therefore to save ourselves from accidents, we needn't try to flee,
For whatsoever God ordained will come to pass
For instance, ye may be killed by a stone or piece of glass.

✺ The Most Anticlimactic Poem ✺

It is no easy task to take a dramatic subject and, through a line of ill-conceived verse, rob it of all drama whatsoever. Yet this is what the very bad poet does. The more advanced very bad poet takes it one step further—writing about a banal subject and descending to the even more banal with a thud.

from *The Grand Rapids Cricket Club*

by *Julia A. Moore*

When Mr. Dennis does well play,
His courage is full great,
And accidents to him occur,
But not much though, of late.

JAMES MCINTYRE

(1827–1906)

A furniture maker by trade, James McIntyre turned his hand to poetry in order to help others appreciate the many wonders of Canada as he viewed them. Key among them: cheese. Few could argue with his rationale; to wit, "it is no insignificant theme."

He also found other Canadian topics to write about, ranging from the appointment of a new whip in the Ontario legislature to bear hunting to an eighteen-foot ox exhibited at a fair. He even plugged his own furniture business in his inimitable style ("McIntyre has a few rows / Of the latest styles of Bureaus"). McIntyre turned out two books of poetry, *Musings on the Banks of Canadian Thames* and *Poems of James McIntyre*— both proof that he was a Canadian original, the North American equivalent of Scottish poet William McGonagall.

As one of his fans wrote, in a letter excerpted in McIntyre's second collection of poems:

> In writing you do not pretend
> With Tennysonian themes to blend,
> It is an independent style
> Begotten on Canadian soil.

The following poem—one of McIntyre's much vaunted "cheese odes"—is about an actual cheese. The particular cheese that merited such waxing weighed four tons and was displayed at a Toronto exposition circa 1855.

Ode on the Mammoth Cheese

Weighing over 7,000 pounds

We have seen thee, queen of cheese,
Lying quietly at your ease,
Gently fanned by evening breeze,
Thy fair form no flies dare seize.

All gaily dressed soon you'll go
To the great Provincial show,
To be admired by many a beau
In the city of Toronto.

Cows numerous as a swarm of bees,
Or as the leaves upon the trees,
It did require to make thee please,
And stand unrivalled, queen of cheese.

May you not receive a scar as
We have heard that Mr. Harris
Intends to send you off as far as
The great world's show at Paris.

Of the youth beware of these,
For some of them might rudely squeeze
And bite your cheek, then songs or glees
We could not sing, oh! queen of cheese.

We'rt thou suspended from balloon,
You'd cast a shade even at noon,
Folks would think it was the moon
About to fall and crush them soon.

These are two more examples of McIntyre's dairy odes—proof that he fully deserved the epithet that was bestowed upon him: "the Cheese Poet."

from *Oxford Cheese Ode*

The ancient poets ne'er did dream
That Canada was land of cream
They ne'er imagined it could flow
In this cold land of ice and snow,
Where everything did solid freeze,
They ne'er hoped or looked for cheese.

Prophecy of a Ten Ton Cheese

In presenting this delicate, dainty morsel to the imagination of the people I believed it could be realized. I viewed the machine that turned and raised the mammoth cheese, and saw the powerful machine invented by James Ireland at the West Oxford companies' factory to turn the great and fine cheese he was making there. This company with but little assistance could produce a ten ton cheese.

Who hath prophetic vision sees
In future times a ten ton cheese,
Several companies would join
To furnish curd for great combine,
More honor far than making gun
Of mighty size and many a ton.

Machine it could be made with ease
That could turn this monster cheese,

The greatest honour to our land
Would be this orb of finest brand,
Three hundred curd that would need squeeze
For to make this mammoth cheese.

So British lands could confederate
Three hundred provinces in one state,
When all in harmony agrees
To be pressed in one like this cheese,
Then one skilful hand could acquire
Power to move British empire.

But various curds must be combined
And each factory their curd must grind,
To blend harmonious in one
This great cheese of mighty span,
And uniform in quality
A glorious reality.

Disaster to Steamer Victoria at London

At London, Thames is a broad stream
Which was the scene of a sad theme.
A fragile steamer there did play
O'ercrowded on a Queen's Birthday,
While all on board was bright and gay;
But soon, 'neath the cold water, lay
Naught but forms of lifeless clay.
Which made, alas! sad month of May.

from *Potato Bug Exterminators*

When we do trace out nature's laws,
And view effects, and muse on cause,
For the future there's great hope
If we our eyes do only ope.
With joy they will often glisten,
If to truth one doth but listen;
But people often turn deaf ear
And what is useful will not hear.

Now for a minute, lend your luggs,
Our theme, it is potato bugs.

Wooden Leg

Misfortune sometimes is a prize,
And is a blessing in disguise;
A man with a stout wooden leg,
Through town and country he can beg.

And the people in the city,
On poor man they do take pity;
He points them to his timber leg
And tells them of his poor wife, Meg.

And if a dog tries him to bite,
With his stiff leg he doth him smite,
Or sometimes he will let him dig
His teeth into the wooden leg.

Then never more will dog delight
This poor cripple man for to bite;
Rheumatic pains they never twig,
Nor corns annoy foot of leg.

So cripple if he's man of sense,
Finds for ill some recompense;
And though he cannot dance a jig,
He merry moves on wooden leg.

And when he only has one foot,
He needs to brush only one boot;
Through world he does jolly peg,
So cheerful with his wooden leg.

In mud or water he can stand
With his foot on the firm dry land,
For wet he doth not care a fig,
It never hurts his wooden leg.

No aches he has but on the toes
Of one foot, and but one gets froze;
He has many a jolly rig,
And oft enjoys his wooden leg.

GEORGE MEREDITH

(1828–1909)

The cerebral English novelist and poet focused much of his in-
tellect on two themes: social Darwinism and the relationships and
battles between the sexes; the latter theme was stimulated by the
author's own bad marriage. Fame came relatively late to the prolific
Meredith, who at his best could be a powerful and amusing social
critic but at his worst could descend into what critics politely call
"artificiality and forced wit."

The following extremely obtuse selection is from a longer ex-
tremely obtuse poem. This particular excerpt concerns a practice
followed at one time by the people of Marseilles to keep the plague
from ravaging them. Each year the people would choose a sacrificial
victim and use public funds to fatten him for the entire year. At the
end of the year the victim would be led through the streets, jeered
at by the public, then pushed off a cliff, in the hopes that the sacri-
fice would keep the plague at bay.

from *The Empty Purse*

A Sermon to Our Later Prodigal Son

He cancelled the ravaging Plague
  With the roll of his fat off the cliff.
Do thou, with thy lean as the weapon of ink,
  Though they call thee an angler who fishes the vague
    And catches none too pink,
Attack one as murderous, knowing thy cause
Is the cause of community. Iterate,
Iterate, iterate, harp on the trite:
Our preacher to win is the supple in stiff:
Yet always in measure with bearing polite:
The manner of one that would expiate.

OWEN MEREDITH
(ROBERT LYTTON, EARL OF LYTTON)

(1831–1891)

As a poet, Lytton is perhaps best described as being first and foremost a diplomat and statesman. The son of Parliament member and writer Edward George Bulwer Lytton, Baron of Lytton, Robert Lytton held a number of diplomatic posts throughout Europe. He topped his career with an ambassadorship in Paris, yet like most members of the diplomatic set, all the while he fervently believed his true talents lay elsewhere.

Lytton thought of himself as a Byronic poet, and he spent much of his free time churning out innumerable verses under the pseudonym "Owen Meredith." His poems were often published in quite handsome editions with steel-cut illustrations to illuminate the more fervid passages. Most of his poems are a blend of romantic flushes, handsome mustachioed lords, heaving bosoms, and quite often a touch of the macabre.

Going Back Again

I dream'd that I walk'd in Italy,
    When the day was going down,
By a water that silently wander'd by
    Thro' an old dim-lighted town,

Till I came to a palace fair to see.
    Wide open the windows were
My love at a window sat; and she
    Beckon'd me up the stair. . . .

When I came to the little rose-colour'd room,
    From the curtains out flew a bat.

The window was open: and in the gloom
    My love at the window sat.

She sat with her guitar on her knee,
    But she was not singing a note,
For someone had drawn (ah, who could it be?)
    A knife across her throat.

from *The Vampyre*

I found a corpse, with golden hair,
    Of a maiden seven months dead.
But the face, with the death in it, still was fair,
    And the lips with their love were red.
    Rose-leaves on a snow-drift shed,
    Blood-drops by Adonis bled,
    Doubtless were not so red.

. . .

I would that this woman's head
    Were less golden about the hair:
I would her lips were less red,
    And her face less deadly fair.
    For this is the worst to hear—
    How came that redness there?

'T is my heart, be sure, she eats for her food;
    And it makes one's whole flesh creep
To think that she drinks and drains my blood
    Unawares, when I am asleep.
    How else could those red-lips keep
    Their redness so damson-deep?

There's a thought like a serpent, slips
    Ever into my heart and head,—
There are plenty of women, alive and human,
    One might woo, if one wished, and wed—
Women with hearts, and brains,—ay, and lips
    Not so very terribly red.

The following country-house soliloquy is also typically Mere-dithian. In this one the bard tries to deftly and lightly contrast the failed love affair of an insect (of the midge genus) with that of a man at a party who has just been deserted by a brilliant woman.

from *Midges*

She is talking aesthetics, the dear clever creature. . . .
    Her ideas are divine upon Art, upon Nature. . . .
I no more am found worthy to join in the talk, now:
    While she leads our poetical friend up the walk, now.

Meanwhile there is dancing in yonder green bower
    A swarm of young midges. They dance high and low.
'Tis a sweet little species that lives but one hour,
    And the eldest was born half an hour ago.

One impulsive young midge I hear ardently pouring
    In the ears of a shy wanton in gauze. . . .
His passion is not, he declares, the mere fever
    Of a rapturous moment. It knows no control:
It will burn in his breast through existence forever,
    Immutably fixed in the deeps of the soul!

She wavers: she flutters: . . . male midges are fickle:
    Dare she trust him her future? . . . she asks with a sigh:

He implores, . . . and a tear is beginning to trickle:
　　She is weak: they embrace, and . . . the lovers pass by.

While they pass me, down here on a rose leaf has lighted
　　A pale midge, his feelers all drooping and torn:
His existence is withered; its future is blighted:
　　His hopes are betrayed: and his breast is forlorn.

By the midge his heart trusted his heart is deceived, now
　　In the virtue of midges no longer he believes. . . .
His friends would console him . . . life is yet before him;
　　Many hundred long seconds he still has to live:

There is Fame! There's Ambition! and grander than either,
　　There is freedom! . . . and the progress and march of
　　　　the race! . . .
But to Freedom his breast beats no longer, and neither
　　Ambition nor action her loss can replace.

If the time had been spent in acquiring aesthetics
　　I have squandered in learning the language of midges,
There might, for my friend in her peripatetics,
　　Have been now *two* asses to help her o'er the bridges.

As it is . . . I'll report to her the whole conversation.
　　It would have been longer; but somehow or other
(In the midst of that misanthrope's long lamentation)
　　A midge in my right eye became a young mother.

Since my friend is so clever, I'll ask her to tell me
　　Why the least living thing (a mere midge in the egg!)
Can make a man's tears flow, as it now befell me. . . .
　　O you dear clever young woman, explain it, I beg!

⊷ The Worst Attempts at Rhymes By Very Bad Poets ⊱

The intrepid very bad poet doesn't let something as simple as not having the right word in mind get in his or her way. Sometimes a bad poet stretches so hard for a rhyme that we as readers are forced to do a little stretching on our own, as in the following prime examples of truly creative attempts at rhyming.

from *In a Book-store*
by *Francis Saltus Saltus*

Sad, on Broadway next afternoon,
I strolled in listless manner,
Humming her most detested tune,
And smoking an Havana.

from *The Light-Bearer of Liberty*
by *J. W. Scholl*

Gooing babies, helpless pygmies,
Who shall solve your Fate's enigmas?

from *Indian Corn*
by *Rev. William Cook*

Corn, corn, sweet Indian corn,
Greenly you grew long ago.
Indian fields well to adorn,
And to parch or grind hah-ho!

JAMES MILLIGAN

(fl. 1800s)

Little is known of the poet, save his obvious love of geology.

from *The Science of Geology*

In ages past [animals] lived and died,
And afterwards were petrified
By enclosure in massive rocks,
And thus became fossilised blocks.
The oldest-known rocks contain lime,
Thus proving at that remote time
Animal life did then abound,
Which may fill us with thought profound.

BERTHA MOORE

(fl. 1890s)

Not much is known about Bertha Moore except that she flourished in Victorian England. Her baby talk poem is not unique; this genre was extremely popular at the end of the last century. The modern discoverer of Moore's baby talk verse found it in Ernest Pertwee's *The Reciter's Second Treasury of Verse,* following, of all things, Adam's morning hymn from Milton's *Paradise Lost.*

A Child's Thought

If I were God, up in the sky,
    I'll tell you all vat I would do,
I would not let the babies cry
    Because veir tooths was coming froo.
I'd make them born wif tooths all white,
    And curly hair upon veir heads
And so vat vey could sit upright
    Not always lie down in veir beds.

If I were God, up in the sky,
    I'd make the sweet primroses talk,
And tell me why vey sometimes sigh,
    When nurse and I close to them walk.
I 'spects it is 'cos vey do fear
    We'll tread upon vem when we run,
But we would not go *quite* so near,
    To kill a primrose is not fun.

If I were God, up in the sky,
    And mummie's head was *bery* bad,
I'd send an angel from on high
    And that would make her, oh! so glad!
She'd beg God let him stay awhile,
    And soon forget the horrid pain,
Talk to the angel, laugh and smile,
    And ven be quite herself again.

If I were God, up in the sky,
    I'd take all nasty little boys
Who play so rough and noisily
    And break veir sister's fav'rite toys.

I'd turn vem into tiny crabs,
    And make vem run about in sand,
And play wif fishes and wif dabs
    P'raps ven vey wouldn't be so grand.

If I were God, up in the sky,
    I'd have so many fings to do,
'Twould be a 'sponsibility.
    I really fink, 'tween me and you,
I'd raver be a little girl,
    Whom Daddy calls his "Precious Pearl."
It's *bery* difficult to try
    To be like God, up in the sky!

JULIA A. MOORE

(1847–1920)

Julia A. Moore, known as "The Sweet Singer of Michigan," was praised by none other than Mark Twain, who said that her first book of poetry gave him joy for twenty years.

That book, *The Sweet Singer of Michigan Salutes the Public* (the title later changed to the more euphonious *A Sentimental Song Book*) was a success and went through three reprints—principally because Twain and others thought it so unintentionally hilarious that they recommended it to friends. Moore took their "praise" quite literally and so encouraged turned out *A Few Choice Words for the Public*.

Moore's recurrent poetic theme was death—particularly violent death through some form of disaster, such as a railway disaster of Ashtabula and a yellow fever epidemic, but also via more prosaic means such as lightning, overturned sleighs, and drowning. Moore was particularly partial to infant mortality, particularly with dead curly blond-haired blue-eyed infants as subjects.

One contemporary critic wrote that Moore was "worse than a

Gatling gun," and came up with a count of casualties in one of Moore's books. The grand total: 21 killed, 9 wounded.

from *Hattie House*

She had blue eyes and light flaxen hair,
  Her little heart was light and gay,
She said to her mother, that morning fair,
  "Mother, can I go out and play?"

She left the house, this dear little girl,
  On that bright and pleasant day—
She went to play with two little girls
  That were near about her age.

. . .

Those little girls will not forget
  The day that Hattie died,
For she was with them when she fell in a fit,
  While playing by their side.

from *Little Libbie*

One morning in April, a short time ago,
  Libbie was active and gay;
Her Saviour called her, she had to go,
  'Ere the close of that pleasant day.

While eating dinner, this dear little child
  Was choked on a piece of beef.
Doctors came, tried their skill awhile,
  But none could give relief.

from *Roll On, Time, Roll On*

Air—"Roll on, Silver Moon"

Some people are getting so they think a poor girl,
    Though she be bright and intelligent and gay,
She must have nice clothes, or she is nothing in this
    world,
    If she is not dressed in style every day.

Remember never to judge people by their clothes,
    For our brave noble Washington said,
"Honorable are rags, if a true heart they enclose,"
    And I found it was the truth when I married.

from *Croquet by Moonlight*

On a moonlight evening, in the month May,
A number of young people were playing at croquet. . . .

. . .

It was a merry party, for lady Dell was there,
Her merry laugh above the rest was heard by all, so fair. . . .
She was the belle of the evening, admired by great and
    small,
And all the boys liked to play with the girl and blue ball.

Two young men among them, that loved this pretty Dell:
Although I write about them, their names I will not tell.
They were fine young fellows, so bashful, and yet so gay;
They tried to beat the girl with the blue ball play.

This is about a steam train disaster on the Ashtabula Bridge, resulting in numerous deaths, which were, of course, carefully catalogued by Moore.

Ashtabula Disaster

Air—"Gently Down the Stream of Time"

Have you heard of the dreadful fate,
    Of Mr. P. P. Bliss and wife?
Of their fate I will relate,
    And also others lost their life;
Ashtabula Bridge disaster,
    Where so many people died
Without a thought that destruction
    Would plunge them 'neath the wheel of tide.

Chorus

Swiftly passed the engine's call
    Hastening souls on to death,
Warning not one of them all;
    It brought despair right and left.

Among the ruins are many friends,
    Crushed to death amidst the roar;
On one thread all may depend,
    And hope they've reached the other shore.

P. P. Bliss showed great devotion
    To his faithful wife, his pride,
When he saw that she must perish,
    He died a martyr by her side. . . .

. . .

Destruction lay on every side,
  Confusion, fire and despair;
No help, no hope, so they died,
  Two hundred people over there.
Many ties was there broken
  Many a heart filled with pain,
Each one left a little token,
  For above they live again.

Hiram Helsel

Once was a boy, age fifteen year,
  Hiram Helsel was his name,
And he was sick two years or so;
  He has left this world of pain. . . .

He was a small boy of his age
  When he was five years or so
Was shocked by lightning while to play,
  It caused him not to grow.
He was called little Hi. Helsel
  By all friends that knew him well—
His life was sad, as you shall hear
  And the truth to you I tell.

from *The Brave Page Boys*

Enos Page the youngest brother—
  His age was fourteen years—
Had five sons in one family
  Went from Grand Rapids here.

In Eight Michigan Cavalry
        This boy he did enlist.
His life was almost despaired of
        On account of numerous fits.

from *The Author's Early Life*

And now, kind friends, what I have wrote,
        I hope you will pass o'er,
And not criticize as some have done,
        Hitherto herebefore.

EDWARD NEWMAN

(fl. 1840)

Edward Newman will probably be remembered best for his *History of British Ferns* and *Introduction to the Study of Insects,* both of which garnered good reviews and sales, going into three and four editions respectively. His less renowned poetry may have been inspired during his many long rambles through the English countryside, presumably studying the aforementioned ferns and insects.

Earwigs

First of walkers come the Earwigs,
Earwigs or FORFICULINA;
At the tail we find a weapon,
Very like a pair of pincers,

And with this 'tis said the Earwigs
Open and fold up the hind wings;
You may watch them and observe it;
I have never had the pleasure.

GEORGIA BAILEY PARRINGTON

(fl. 1907)

Parrington won accolades on the basis of only one poem: "An
Elegy to a Dissected Puppy," an antivivisection piece that captures
the reader from the very first line. The *New York Evening Post* praised
the poet as "the latest addition to the galaxy of the Tar Heel State"
and recognized her poetry as "a thing of merit . . . not to be lost."

Unfortunately, the complete poem *has* been lost. Only the fol-
lowing stanzas remain. However the *Evening Post* does give readers
a tantalizing hint of the close of the poem. The dog is dead, but
Parrington imagines it living again "mayhap in far-off hunting
grounds, on aerial feet."

from *An Elegy to a Dissected Puppy*

Sweet Dog! now cold and stiff in death,
    What cruel hand enticed thee here?
Did toothsome crust of juicy bone
    Allure to stretch on thy bier?

. . . ruthless hands of alien race
    Are opening up thy quiet breast,
With prying eyes they peer within,
    Explore the contents of thy chest.

ROBERT PETER

(fl. 1800s)

On Time, Death, and Eternity

But ah! when first to breathe man does begin
He then inhales the noxious seeds of sin,
Which every goodly feeling does destroy
And more or less his after life annoy.

≈§ The Worst Tribute to a Great Poet ิ≈

Many bad poets have paid tribute to the greats of their profession, usually in appropriately atrocious verse. Shelley is the victim in the lines below.

from *English Poets*

by *James McIntyre*

Shelley

We have scarcely time to tell thee
Of the strange and gifted Shelley,
Kind hearted man, but ill-fated,
So youthful drowned and cremated.

MATTIE J. PETERSON

(1866–1947) or (1866–1906)

Peterson's life was the stuff of a sentimental novel, quite possibly much like the one she wrote. A North Carolina native, she spent her early life at home, too disabled to attend school. Her rather dismal home life inspired her to write a little-read novel, *Little Pansy*, but it was her decision to append eleven poems at the end of the novel that brought her world acclaim. A local editor championed her poems, which he and other critics said rivaled those of Julia A. Moore (q.v.).

As for the life of the poet, one account says she died in 1906; another suggests she grew up and became a lonely schoolteacher who then became a mail-order bride in Texas and died at the ripe old age of eighty-one after eating a rather large watermelon.

I Kissed Pa Twice after His Death

I kissed dear Pa at the grave,
    Then soon he was buried away;
Wreaths were put on his tomb,
    Whose beauty soon decay. . . .

. . .

I saw him coming stepping high,
    Which was of his walk the way;
I had stopped at a house near by—
    His face was as pale as clay. . . .

. . .

When he was having convulsions
    He feared he would hurt me;
Therefore told me to go away.
    He had dug artichokes for me.

Pa dug artichokes on that day,
    He never will dig any more;
He has only paid the debt we owe,
    We should try to reach the shining shore.

Here Peterson reminisces nostalgically about the charms of her rural southern home.

from *The Old Homestead*

. . . I sometimes alligators heard
    When I was on the piazza at home;
Ma, also their noise heard,
    Which was generally in the gloom;
Brother Jimmie and his brother one killed
    And brought it to the house near;
I beheld it in death still,
    But the monster was not fair.

. . .

The red haw grows at the old home,
    Which is sweeter than the river haw;
But the river haw has a perfume
    Which is nice in the nostril to draw.

JAMES HENRY POWELL

(fl. 1850)

Not much is known of this poet, who published several books of verse, including *The Village Bridal, and Other Poems* as well as *Phases of Thought*.

Lines Written for a Friend on the Death of His Brother, Caused by a Railway Train Running over Him Whilst He Was in a State of Inebriation

How oft alas my brother have I warned thee to beware
The horrid spells of guilt which led the drunkards' life to
    care;
But no! you heeded not the warning words I spoke with
    pain,
Your wretched soul that once was pure was bound as in a
    chain;
At length, one cold October, when the night was late and
    dark,
The awful doom came on which sank thy life's unsteady
    barque;
Thy mangled corpse upon the rails in frightful shape was
    found,
The ponderous train had killed thee as its heavy wheels
    went round.

JAMES WHITCOMB RILEY

(1849–1916)

James Whitcomb Riley, known as the "Hoosier poet," was the most popular American writer of his time, and certainly the wealthiest.

Riley began writing after first trying his hand at a range of odd jobs. He was an itinerant sign painter and an actor working with patent medicine shows until he took up with the *Indianapolis Journal* and began writing dialect poems. The public adored them. From then on Riley was a rousing success, turning out favorites such as "When the Frost Is on the Punkin," "Little Orphant Annie," and "The Raggedy Man."

The secret of Riley's success seems to have been the combination of sentimental, homey subjects with a homespun philosophy—and often a heavy touch of Hoosier dialect, heavy on slang and apostrophes and light on grammar and final *g*s. Only Riley could write lines such as "Good's 'bout 'leventy-hunnerd times better than gold!" Perhaps only Riley would want to.

The Smitten Purist

And the Charming Miss Smith's Effect upon Him

Thweet Poethy! let me *lithp* forthwith,
That I may thhing of the name of Smith—
    Which name, alath!
    In Harmony hath
No adequate rhyme, letht you grant me thith—
That the thimple thibillant thound of eth—
(Which to thave my thoul, I can not expreth!)
    Thuth I may thhingingly,
    Wooingly and winningly
    Thu—thu—thound in the name of Smith.

O give me a name that will rhyme with Smith,—
For wild and weird ath the sthrange name ith,
  I would sthrangle a sthrain
  And a thad refrain
Faint and sthweet ath a whithpered kissth;
I would thhing thome thong for the mythic mitth
Who beareth the thingular name of Smith—
  The dathzling brilli-ant
  Rarely rethilliant
  Ap-pup-pellation of Smith!

O had I a name that would rhyme with Smith—
Thome rhythmical tincture of rethonant blith—
  Thome melody rare
  Ath the cherubth blare
On them little trumpeth they're foolin' with—
I would thit me down, and I'd thhing like thith
Of the girl of the thingular name of Smith—
  The sthrangely curiouth,
  Rich and luxuriouth
  Pup-patrronymic of Smith.

from *The Happy Little Cripple*

I'm thist a little crippled boy, an' never goin' to grow
An' git a great big man at all! —'cause Aunty told me so.
When I was this a baby onc't I falled out of the bed
An' got "The Curv'ture of the Spine"—'ats what the
  Doctor said.
I never had no Mother nen—fer my Pa runned away
An' dassn't come back here no more—'cause he was drunk
  one day

An' stobbed a man in thish-ere town, an' couldn't pay his
fine!
An' nen my Ma she died—an' I got "Curv'ture of the
Spine"!

I'm nine years old! an' you can't guess how much I weigh,
I bet!
Last birthday I weighed thirty three! An' I weigh thirty
yet!
I'm awful little for my size—I'm purt' nigh littler 'an
Some babies is!—an' neighbors all calls me "The Little
Man!"
An' Doc one time he laughed and said: "I 'spect, first thing
you know,
You'll have a spike-tail coat an' travel with a show!"
An' nen I laughed—till I looked round an' Aunty was a-
cryin'—
Sometimes she acts like that, 'cause I got "Curv'ture of the
Spine!"

from *A Dubious "Old Kriss"*

Us-folks is purty pore—but Ma
She's waitin'—two years more—tel Pa
He serves his term out. Our Pa he—
He's in the Penitenchurie!

Now don't you tell!—'cause *Sis,*
The baby, *she* don't know he is—
'Cause she wuz only four, you know,
He kissed her last an' hat to go!

Pa alluz liked Sis best of all
Us childern.—'Spect it's 'cause she fall
When she 'us ist a *chiled,* one day—
An' make her back look thataway.

Pa—'fore he be a burglar—he's
A locksmiff, an' maked locks, an' keys,
An' knobs you pull for bells to ring,
An' he could ist make *anything!*

'Cause our Ma *say* he can!—*An'* this
Here little pair of crutches Sis
Skips round on—Pa maked *them*—yessir!—
An' silvur-plate-name here for her!

Pa's out o' work when Chris'mus come
One time, an' stay away from home,
An' 's drunk an' 'buse our Ma, an' swear
They ain't no "Old Kriss" anywhere!

AMANDA MCKITTRICK ROS

(1860–1939)

In the 1890s Amanda McKittrick Ros began amazing audiences with her novels, all of which bore alliterative titles such as *Irene Iddesleigh,* and *Donald Dudley.* These were soon followed by Ros's equally alliteratively titled books of verse: *Poems of Puncture* and *Fumes of Formation,* which Ros explains was

> hatched within a mind fringed with Fumes of Forma-
> tion, the Ingenious Innings of Inspiration and Thorny
> Tincture of Thought.

Ros applied those "Ingenious Innings of Inspiration" to transform her own rather prosaic life in Northern Ireland. She dropped the extra *s* from her husband's last name of Ross, probably to link herself to the ancient family of de Ros; claimed that the McKittricks were descended from King Sitric of Denmark; and elevated her beloved husband to friendship with the eminent Victorian leader Sir Randolph Churchill, who apparently once happened to pass through her husband's train station.

Ros was famous for her bizarre word usage. She coined such descriptive terms as "sanctified measures of time" (Sunday), "globes of glare" (eyes), "bony supports" (legs), "southern necessary" (pants—*south* refers to the southern or lower portion of the body) and "globules of liquid lava" (sweat).

Although not the "high-bred daughter of distinguished effeminacy" she wished to have been, Ros was something else: a writer with a gift for (as she puts it) "disturbing the bowels."

On Visiting Westminster Abbey

A "Reduced Dignity" invited me to muse on its merits

> Holy Moses! Have a look!
> Flesh decayed in every nook!
> Some rare bits of brain lie here
> Mortal loads of beef and beer,
> Some of whom are turned to dust,
> Every one bids lost to lust
>
> . . .
>
> Famous some were—yet they died;
> Poets—Statesmen—Rogues beside,
> Kings—Queens, all of them do rot,
> What about them? Now—they're not!

A Little Belgian Orphan

Daddy was a Belgian and so was Mammy too,
And why I'm now in Larne I want to tell to you:
Daddy was a soldier and fought his level best
For both his King and Country, and I'll tell you the rest.
Our home was snug and cosy and how happy we were all,
Until Daddy he was ordered to obey his country's call. . . .

. . .

One day a short time after, a troop of Germans came,
While we sat around the table, playing a childish game;
Mammy was busy baking bread for all our tea,
When the door was flung wide open and in stepped Ger-
    mans three.
One spoke to Mammy saying, "Stay your labour for your
    kids,
Give to us all this bread! or we'll stab your bony ribs!"
And raising high his glittering sword one cut off Mammy's
    head,
Her body fell upon me, while her poor neck bled and
    bled!

Three shots soon followed after, and my dear wee brothers
    three
Fell dead across poor Mammy whose neck bled on my
    knee;
I screamed, "Oh sirs, wee Hors is shot, and Buhn and Wil-
    helm too!"
Then on my knees I fell and begged they'd spare wee
    brother Dhu;

Just then they raised the little lad and threw him on the fire,
And wreathed in smiles they watched him burn until he
    did expire;
My poor wee sisters screamed and cried, and clutched
    dead Mammy's hands,
When lo! they cut off baby's head and also her wee hands.

. . .

Ah sirs, I begged, just kill me now, else I shall die with
    fear. . . .
One drew his sword—cut off my hand, I reached the
    other out,
"Cut this off too, ye cowards?" I then began to shout.
In rushed some neighbour women with knives both bright
    and sharp
And stabbed the Kaiser's butchers into their very hearts.

. . .

Take warning all ye British Boys, turn out in thousands
    strong;
Go fight for King and Country and France will aid you on!
If you should meet the Kaiser, cut off his only arm,
For his "wee one," it won't matter, it can't do any harm.

I've just heard Daddy, too, is killed, so all alone I'm left,
Of brothers, sisters, parents dear, I have been made
    bereft. . . .
Some day I'll die and meet them all, 'twill be a joyous
    sight,
For us to live in glory, and view the Kaiser's plight—
Tortured with remorseful flames, he won't have power to
    quell
If nobody conquer him on earth the devil will in ———.

This poem is written of a visit to the cemetery ("tracks of lifeless friends" is Rosian for "cemetery"). It is particularly notable for the confused speculation at the end.

Thoughts

No place I love to visit more
 Than tracks of lifeless friends,
For, when I weary grow, I go
 To study odds and ends. . . .

The great, the mighty, medium, poor
 In that one flat do lie
In abject silence, ne'er they spake
 No matter how they try.
Some marble symbols which record,
 The virtues of the dead
Are like all lawyers in a court,
 Who truthful clients dread. . . .

Wherein like many of the poor
 With tiny bits of slate
Stuck round in every shape and form
 Apart from rich and great. . . .

Each slate records the name and age,
 Where he or she was laid,
Scored thereon with a gravel stone
 Which rock their debts have paid.
Alas! Upon that Mighty Day,
 All grades—all sects must rise,
What if the poor the rich shall be
 Before poor Riches' eyes!

This is a polemic against Ros's most noted critic, Barry Pain, at the announcement of his death.

The End of "Pain"

That Pain has ceased to mock, to mar
Those gems he picked up near and far,
Is evident. His pricky pen
Reclaim it ne'er shall he again
A mighty maggot, he thought he,
A slavey now to Master D.

. . .

Great Mercy! I shall say no more
But ask and answer as of yore:
Why should all such "rodents of State"
Have scope to nibble—genius great?
The answer is—They're bare of bread
Their only food—a brilliant head.

Although the title suggests otherwise, this poem is a polemic against modern fashion, and, in the poet's unspoken last word, against, as she might put it, "s——x."

The Old Home

By a freak of the lustful that spreads like a disease
Which demanded that females wear pants if you please,
But I stuck to the decentest of attire
And to alter my "gender" I'll never aspire.

During that hallowed century now dead and gone
In which good Queen Victoria claimed to be born:
From childhood her modesty was seen
Her exalted position demanded when Queen.

She set an example of decency rare,
That no English Queen before her you'd compare:
Neither nude knee nor ankle, nude bosom nor arm
Dare be seen in her presence this Queen to alarm.

She believed in her sex being loving and kind,
And modesty never to march out of line
By exposing those members unrest to achieve,
Which pointed to morals immorally grave.

But said to relate when she bade "Adieu"
To earth and its vanities tainted with "rue"
That centre of fashion, so French in its style.
Did its utmost to vilify decency's smile.

. . .

It wasn't long after till modesty grew
A thing of the past for me and for you;
Last century's fashions were blown quite aside,
The ill-advised folk of this age now deride.

The petticoat faded away as we do
In circumference it covered not one leg but two,
Its successor exposes the arms, breasts and necks,
Legs, knees and thighs and too often—the ———.

On a Girl Who Took Action for Breach of Promise

She rises mostly every day,
At sunrise, noon or night,
Her one and only thought is where's
The drink to make her "tight."
For it very often happens,
That bipeds so inclined
Would practise tricks more filthy
Than drinking too much wine.

. . . [her lips] form the sweetest mouth e'er made
   Void of that horrid smell
Of cigs, so many female grades
   Prefer to Heaven or ————!

The following lines criticize modern women who have picked up
bad masculine habits.

from *I Love to See a Lady Nice and Natural at Any Price*

And smoke and spit, no matter where,
And very often curse and swear,
I lose my temper o'er these arts
That stamp such women—Dirty Clarts.

✍ When Bad Poems Happen ✑
to Good Poets

William Wordsworth, one of England's greatest poets, poet laureate of England, author of numerous masterpieces, had his off days. Sometimes it was just a line that went astray—as in his unconsciously pornographic:

> Give me your tool, to him I said.

Other times it was an entire poem, such as the following work—possibly one of the worst poems ever written by a good poet. Wordsworth explained that he was compelled to write these lines after seeing

> on a stormy day, a thorn which I had often past, in
> calm and bright weather, without noticing it. I said
> to myself, "Cannot I by some invention do as much
> to make this Thorn permanently an impressive object
> as the storm has made it to my eyes at the moment?

Unfortunately for Wordsworth, many might say that the answer to his question is no.

from *The Thorn*
by *William Wordsworth*

Before you up the mountain go,
Up to the dreary mountain-top,
I'll tell you all I know.
'Tis now some two-and-twenty years
Since she (her name is Martha Ray)
Gave, with a maiden's true good will,
Her company to Stephen Hill;
And she was blithe and gay,
And she was happy, happy still
Whene'er she thought of Stephen Hill.

And they had fixed the wedding day,
The morning that must wed them both;
But Stephen to another Maid
Had sworn another oath;
And with the other Maid, to church
Unthinking Stephen went—
Poor Martha! on that woeful day
A cruel, cruel fire, they say,
Into her bones was sent:
It dried her body like a tinder,
And almost turned her brain to cinder.

FRANCIS SALTUS SALTUS

(1849–1889)

American poet Francis Saltus Saltus considered himself a member of the decadent school of literature. He loved modern women who smoked cigarettes, and he pored through the Bible in search of pornographic sections and idolized the French writers Baudelaire, Gerard de Nerval, and the Marquis de Sade.

Like his heroes, Saltus was fascinated by the morbid, the depraved, and the abnormal. Unlike them he wrote with a boyish exuberance—especially heavy on the exclamation points—and this tendency adds a novel twist to his theoretically dark poetic subjects.

By the time Saltus died at age thirty-nine, he had written over five thousand poems, most of them a unique blend of lurid subject matter, florid imagery, unbridled enthusiasm, and surprise endings—a fascinating collection of "decadence lite."

Here the poet compares British and Indian child-rearing habits, coming to a decidedly anti-multicultural climax.

Mothers

Radiant with vernal grace and summer flowers,
    The English landscape in rich splendor glows;
Half hidden 'mid sweet labyrinths of bowers,
    A snow-white cottage nestles like a rose.

Within a woman sits, supremely blessed.
    Her clear, blue eyes reflect a boundless joy.
When, with long kisses on a loving breast,
    She soothes to sleep her little, dimpled boy!

Delhi's majestic temples, domed and porched,
    Tower up in proud, magnificent array;
The sluggish Ganges, by the fierce sun scorched,
    Gleams like a scimitar in the hot mid-day.

A woman kneels among the reeds and sands,
    Kissing a wee, bronzed child that coos and smiles.
Enough,—great Brahma speaks!—with trembling
    hands
    She hurls her first-born to the crocodiles!

Posthumous Revenge

The one I loathed, my one malignant foe,
    He who had marred my life in cruel wise,
Lay mute before me, nevermore to rise,
    Pierced to his treacherous heart by one quick blow.

. . .

And then, oh God! while I stood fearless there,
    Alone in that deserted, sullied place,
I heard, I heard, a murmur of despair,
    A hot, swift *something* struck me on the face!

Pallid with anger, I did quickly turn,
    To cruelly chastise the foe unknown,
I felt the warm wound on my forehead burn,
    But, oh! avenging God! *we were alone!*

Then horror held me, while I no thing saw,
    I sank unto my knees without control,
For I had understood at last, in awe,
    That what had struck me was his *outraged soul!*

The Kiss

Incorrigible, false coquette,
    She spurned my love and with a smile,
Bade me her promises forget;
    Toying with glittering rings the while.
      (But tell it not.)

. . .

"If it must be, if cherished bliss,
    Is lost to me forever," I cried,
"Give me one last, sweet, parting kiss,
    To soothe my passion's injured pride."
      (But tell it not.)

With pretty gestures like a bird
    In her rare loveliness unique,
She, smiling, rose, without a word,
    And gently kissed my lips and cheek.
      (But tell it not.)

That peerless beauty, chaste and proud,
    Lies in her sumptuous coffin now!
Her sweet limbs hidden in a shroud,
    With spotless lilies on her brow.
      (But tell it not.)

Friend, there are ways of pain and dread
    To veil youth's dawn in sad eclipse;
She could not see the *poison spread*
    On my pale cheeks and livid lips!
      (But tell it not.)

This selection shows Saltus at his cynical best—exposing the worst traits of human nature in the person of a circus ringmaster.

from *The Masters*

1.—A Circus Master Speaks to the Clowns

... Come! show your jolly tricks, and be possessed
  Like devils with mad laughter!
  What are you crying after?
Your child is dead? Bah! Jump right in the ring.
A whining clown forsooth's a silly thing.
  Turn twenty hand-springs right away,
  Or else, by God! I'll stop your pay.

from *Two Loves Found Refuge*
A Mood of Madness

Two loves found refuge in my happy heart,
One for my bride, one for the healing art;
Each of my spirit claimed an equal part.

. . .

But, as my talent rose and waxed mature,
Love for my bride became more insecure,
Love for anatomy more deep and pure.

. . .

She was a *subject* to my eyes alone;
Not woman, forsooth, but so much flesh and bone,
Sinew, and blood, and skin, which were my own.

And I had lawful right, with foul intent,
I who for progress on this sphere was sent,
To use her body for experiment.

So in her wine I dropped consuming blight,
One moaning, shadow-haunted winter night,
And, watching, clutched my scalpel's handle tight.

Then, ere her eyes, that agony expressed,
Had closed forever, with impatient zest,
My hands were red dissecting her white breast.

GEORGE ROBERT SIMS

(1847–?)

A popular playwright, poet, and essayist, George R. Sims was especially noted for his letters to the *Times* on the condition of the poor in London, which sparked a Royal Commission to study the problem, so beginning the never-ending series of government commissions studying urban poverty.

from *Beauty and the Beast*

He gazed on the face of the high-born maid,
And saw the mark where the tears had been;
He knew that a daughter had wept and prayed,

He knew that a mother had feared a scene—
Had torn herself from the weeping girl,
Whose love was away o'er the distant sea,
And had sold her child to a titled churl
Who had just got round from a bad d.t.

SLOCUM SLUGS, ESQ.

(fl. 1857)

Little is known of the poet who wrote "I Saw Her in Cabbage Time" but his alliterative pen name—Slocum Slugs, Esq. Published in the Greensboro (North Carolina) *Patriot and Flag,* March 27, 1857, this poem is probably one of the few American poems about the time-honored task of cutting sauerkraut . . . and certainly one of the most compelling.

I Saw Her in Cabbage Time

A Dutch Melody

I saw her first in Cabbage time,
    She was a-cutting kraut—
She'd stop the cutter, now and then,
    To turn the head about;
And as she'd salt it in a tub
    And stamp it down awhile,
Upon her fresh and rosy lip
    Reposed a witching smile.

I saw her next in Winter time,
    And still she gaily smiled;

For there upon the cooking-stove
　　Her grub was being boiled;
Around the huge and greasy pot,
　　The steam came pouring out;
And from the smell I knew that she
　　Was cooking "speck" and kraut.

When next I saw her, in the Spring,
　　She smiled not as before;
A heavy weight was on her heart—
　　The kraut was "all no more!"
The pot she used to cook it in
　　Was eaten up with rust;
The cutter hung upon the wall
　　'Mid spider webs and dust.

WILLIAM B. TAPPAN

(1794–1849)

At the age of thirty-two, the Reverend William B. Tappan entered
the service of the American Sunday School Union, and he contin-
ued working for them until he died. During this time, however, he
also wrote poetry, over twelve volumes' worth. As one might expect
given his affiliation, his poems are all of unflagging moral rectitude
commingled with enthusiastic, even bouncy, zeal. Tappan was prone
to sermonizing in his verse, especially about such topics as the evils
of alcohol. But even he succumbed to temptation when it came to
the retelling of horrific disasters. He let his hair down by writing
turgid poems such as his "Burning of the Orphan Asylum," which
talks about the "dear innocents—who fed the funeral pyre." Yet the
ever-sermonizing Tappan was always sure to find the moral issue
hidden in a tragedy—and blatantly point it out to his readers.

Obey Your Parents

Two brothers once, of merry mood,
   Were sporting in their simple play,
When, chafed and furious from the wood,
   A lion roared against his prey.

Between them and the help they claimed,
   Was interposed a lofty wall;
And hark! beyond it, each is named—
   It is the anxious father's call:

"O, children haste! ye shall not fail
   Of safety with your sire and friend";
"Folly," said one, "for us to scale
   Yon stones, which men can scarce ascend."

"See you not that so rough the path,
   So high the wall, its topmost stone
Ere we could gain, the beast in wrath,
   Might rend and break us bone by bone."

"I," said the other, "come what may,
   Will not despise our father's call;
     'T is safest always to obey,—
       I'll strive to climb yon lofty wall."

He ran, and saw, when drawing nigh,
   A *ladder* reaching from its height;
Safe now, he turned a wistful eye,
   His mangled brother met his sight.

from *Song of the Three Hundred Thousand*
Drunkards in the United States

Onward! though ever in our march,
    Hang Misery's countless train;
Onward for hell—from rank to rank
    Pass we the cup again!

We come! we come! to fill our graves,
    On which shall shine no star;
To glut the worm that never dies—
    Hurrah! hurrah! hurrah!

from *The Last Drunkard*

He stood, the last—the last of all
    The ghastly, guilty band,
Whose clanking chains and cry of thrall
    Once rang throughout the land.

. . .

A sound of moral agony;
    Upon his ear it fell;
A bitter and undreamed of cry,
    With mingled laugh of hell.

. . .

It calls him! and, probation past,
    He shouts, "Ye Fiends, I come!
Open, foul pit, and take the last,
    The last doomed slave of Rum!"

REV. SAMUEL WESLEY SR.

(1660–1735)

The Reverend Samuel Wesley the elder is possibly best known as the father of John Wesley, the founder of Methodism. But Rev. Samuel Wesley deserves to be remembered in his own right—even though his publisher (and friend), John Dunton, noted that "those that allow of no second-rate in [poetry] have endeavoured to lessen his reputation."

Although Wesley mainly wrote on religious topics, his first volume was much more esoteric. Published in 1685, it had the intriguing title *Maggots, or Poems on Several Subjects Never Before Handled*. Among the poems included are "On a Cow's Tail," "Three Skipps of a Louse," and "A Tame Snake Left in a Box of Bran Was Devoured by Mice after a Great Battle"—subjects happily bearing out the promise of the volume's title.

from *On Two Souldiers Killing One Another for a Groat*

Full doleful Tales have oft been told,
By Chimney warm in Winter cold,
About the Sacred Thirst for Gold;
    To hear em half 'twould mad ye.

To Jayl how many Headlong run,
How many a hopeful Youth's undone,
How many a vile ungracious Son
    For this has murder'd Daddy?

from *A Pindaricque on the Grunting of a Hog*

Freeborn Pindaric never does refuse,
Either a lofty, or a humble muse. . . .
Now out of sight she flys,
Roving with gaudy Wings,
A-cross the stormy skys,
Then down again,
Her self she Flings,
Without uneasiness, or Pain
To Lice, and Dogs,
To Cows, and Hogs,
And follows their melodious grunting
o'er the Plain.

. . .

Harmonious Hog draw near!
  No bloody Butchers here,
  Thou need'st not fear.
Harmonious Hog draw near, and from they beauteous
  Snowt,
  Whilst we attend with Ear
  Like thine prik't up devout,
To taste thy sugry Voice, which hear, and there,
With wanton Curls, Vibrates around the Circling Air,
Harmonious Hog! Warble some Anthem out!

CORNELIUS WHUR

(1782–1853)

Cornelius Whur claimed he lived a rather eventful life—but the few particulars known about his life seem to indicate the opposite. A Wesleyan minister, Whur filled his time with work, pottering about the countryside, and talking with a female "bosom companion."

In 1837 he produced his first volume of poems, *Village Musings on Moral and Religious Subjects.* His sentimental poetic ramblings were very well received by local clergy and friends in the area, and the book went through three printings. The good reverend was so encouraged that he penned another volume, with the rather long title *Gratitude's Offering, Being Original Productions on a Variety of Subjects,* which appeared in 1845.

As one can see from the following selections, his "musings" were often a bit macabre—centering on such topics as mutilation, poisoning, graveyards, and death in general.

This poem is said to have been inspired when the good reverend saw an artist who had been born without arms and who earned a living for himself and his family by painting.

from *The Armless Artist*

Alas! Alas! the father said,
O what a dispensation!
How can we be by mercy led,
In such a situation?
Be not surprised at my alarms,
The dearest boy is without arms!

I have no hope, no confidence,
The scene around is dreary;

How can I meet such vast expense?
I am by trying weary.
You must, my dearest, plainly see
This armless boy will ruin me.

This excerpt from a long, dull poem on a walking stick provides a unique allusion to death by poisonous mushroom.

from *The Unfortunate Gentleman*

. . . [I]n a dark and trying hour
(Man hath his days of woe!)
He found in vegetable power
A dreadful, deadly foe!

ELLA WHEELER WILCOX

(1850–1919)

The Times of London called this American "the most popular poet of either sex or age, read by thousands who never opened Shakespeare." Unlike Shakespeare, Wilcox wrote her first book at age ten, and throughout her life she wrote at least two poems a day.

"I think," the vigorous poetess once said, "the word 'poetess' to the average American, until recent years, suggested a sentimental person with ringlets and an absence of practical good sense." Early on, Wilcox set out to disprove this notion, realizing that popular poetry could be turned into cold, hard cash which could buy such delightful things as Connecticut beach houses.

So she churned out poem after poem, dispensing enthusiastic good advice with a late Victorian air. "Do not thrust upon a man's mind continually the idea that you are a vastly higher order of being than he is," she once wrote in a book of advice for women. "He will reach your standard much sooner if you come half-way and meet him on the plane of common sense and human understanding." It was on this plane that Wilcox operated—and earned—so well.

from *Drops of Water*

And he held me fast, and he said, "At last
    I claim thee as mine—all mine."
But I turned my face from love's embrace,
    For the dew on his lips was *wine.*

Then he mounted his steed, and he rode indeed
    Like a knight of the old crusade;
And he wedded soon, e'er the fall of the moon,
    A queenly and haughty maid;
And he drank up his health, and drank up his wealth,
    And his youth, and strength and grace
And now bereft, he has nothing left
    But a bloated, hideous face.

During World War I Wilcox read her poems to soldiers on the Western Front—including the following work, a stirring call to soldiers at war to resist temptation in the form of other women and return to their loved ones at home with a clean "sword." The reaction of the troops is not known.

Come Back Clean

This is the song for a soldier
To sing as he rides from home
To the fields afar where the battles are
Or over the ocean's foam:
"Whatever the dangers waiting
In the lands I have not seen,
If I do not fall—if I come back at all,
Then I will come back clean.

"I may lie in the mud of the trenches,
I may reek with blood and mire,
But I will control, by the God in my soul,
The might of my man's desire.
I will fight my foe in the open,
But my sword shall be sharp and keen
For the foe within who would lure me to sin,
And I will come back clean."

GEORGE WITHER

(1588–1667)

George Wither was one of the most important poets of his time, known widely for his love poems, hymns, and satirical works. His poetry fell out of favor during the Restoration, yet interest in him revived when literary notables such as Charles Lamb and Robert Southey praised his work. Alexander Pope referred to him as "wretched Wither." Many other people, both in his time and later, were also less impressed with Wither. This opinion may have saved Wither's life. As the story, possibly apocryphal, has it, Wither was captured by Royalists during the English Civil War and slated for execution. But Royalist poet Sir John Denham asked the king to spare Wither's life. When asked why, Denham replied, "Because that so long as Wither lived, Denham would not be accounted the worst poet in England."

The following lines lend credence to a comment in England's *Dictionary of National Biography* about Wither's work: "It usually lacks any genuine literary quality and often sinks into imbecilic doggerel."

A Love Sonnet

I loved a lass, a fair one,
    As fair as e'er was seen,
She was indeed a rare one,
    Another Sheba queen
But fool as then I was,
    I thought she loved me too;
But now, alas! sh' 'as left me,
    Falero, lero, loo.

Her hair like gold did glister,
    Each eye was like a star;
She did surpass her sister,
    Which passed all others far.
She would me honey call;
    She'd, O she'd kiss me too,
But now, alas! sh' 'as left me.
    Falero, lero, loo.

POEMS BY UNKNOWN AUTHORS

This poem originally appeared in the Fayetteville *North Carolinian* on February 21, 1857. Although the poet is unknown, apparently he or she chose a subject very near and dear to the hearts of local residents, namely a ditch. This particular ditch was a local landmark, known for its strong smell of sewage and collection of interesting debris. As the *North Carolinian* stated only two months earlier, "that celebrated ditch in our vicinity is now in first-rate skating order—the only inconvenience being a bone sticking up here and there."

Ode to a Ditch

Oh, ditch of all ditches,
Death's store-house of riches,
Where wan disease slumbers mid festoons of slime!
Oh, dark foetid sewer
Where death is the brewer
And *ail* is the liquor he brews all the time!

Oh, hot-bed of fever,
That fatal bereaver
Whose fiery breath blights the blossom of life!
Oh, palace of miasm
Whose hall is a chasm
Where pestilence revels and poison is rife!

Where, where on the earth,
From the place of Sol's birth
To the couch of his rest in the cloud-curtained West,
Is a ditch full as thou

Of the treasures which now
The phantom king hides in thy green oozy breast?

. . .

Oh, wonderful sewer,
Each year brings a newer
And ghostlier charm to thy cavernous deeps!
More puppies and cats,
To say nothing of rats,
And offal and filth of all manner in heaps.

Another dental poem, written in a less learned vein than the
great dental work "Dentologia,"—this particular selection was writ-
ten in the 1890s by an unknown American poet who obviously had
a facility for vivid imagery.

My Last Tooth

You have gone, old tooth,
Though hard to yield,
You have long stood alone,
Like a stub in the field.

Farewell, old tooth . . .
That tainted my breath,
And tasted as smells
A woodpecker's nest.

The following selection is from the 1890s, when a poet's topic of
choice was death, and apparently strolling around the graveyard was
a wonderful way to spend the afternoon.

[*Untitled*]

There is a greater charm to me,
   The wondrous chiseled diction
That on a moss-grown slab we see,
   Than reading modern fiction.

   Although the poet of the following work is unknown, his goal was clear. He hoped not only to render biblical events in verse but also to interpret biblical events in light of more mundane—and scientific—knowledge. He accomplished his aim through the use of the innovative device of the explanatory (and often befuddling) footnote in the body of the poem.

Battles of Joshua

Lest Poets paint each Jewish saint
   And all his deeds declare:
Not one we find amongst mankind
   With Joshua can compare. . . .

  . . .

O'er Gideon's top he made it [the Sun] stop;*
   He also made the moon
Afraid to run and leave the sun;
   She stood o'er Adjalon.

*[Had the Lord informed Moses and Joshua that the sun is the centre of the Solar System, and that there are seven primary and eighteen secondary planets revolving around it; and that Jupiter is more than a thousand times larger than this earth, and has four moons; and that Saturn is several hundred times the size of our globe, and has seven moons; then these favourites of the Lord might have imparted this information to the human race as an important portion of divine revelation; the truths of which would have been confirmed by subsequent discoveries; and the Christian church would not have persecuted people for defending those truths made known by the demonstration of philosophers.]

Those who rely on God defy
All unbelievers, when
The war's begun; for only one
Shall chase a thousand men.*

*[One man of you shall chase a thousand, for the Lord your God he is that fighteth for you. Thus saith the book of Joshua, xxiii, 10. And in the book of Judges we find that one man actually slew a thousand men, with no other weapon than a bone, picked up on the occasion. Such doings in our time would be considered very strange.]

Brave Joshua when he lost some men
Was filled with grief profound;
So great his woes he tore his clothes,
And fell upon the ground.*

*[It was somewhat singular that so great a conqueror as Joshua should have been so distressed at the loss of thirty-six of his own men. But so it was; he rent his clothes, and fell to the earth upon his face. . . . he and all the elders of Israel expressed their grief by putting dust upon their heads. This custom of the Lord's people appears to us as rather singular. In our time people are more inclined to express their feelings of grief and perplexity by scratching the head than by putting dust or dirt upon it.]

. . . These tales of Josh are true, by Gosh,
As any saint can wish,
None can relate accounts more straight
Of Jonah and the fish.

This poem was discovered in a collection of essays and poems, *Interludes,* by a Cambridge scholar, Sir George Otto Trevylan, published in 1905 but written during the author's service as a secretary to his father in British India in 1863.

The author says the poem was "composed by a friend who is passionately devoted to the Laws of Sanitation and Mortality. He carries his enthusiasm on the subject so far as to tinge with it his view of every conceivable matter, religious, political, and literary." The poet's passionate interest in things sanitary is indeed obvious, but even more so is his passion for medical statistics, which renders the poem unique.

[Untitled]

I

. . . I watch the sanitary state,
Jot down of deaths the annual rate,
And each new epidemic greet
Until my system I complete
    Of tropical statistics.

II

Of those with whom I laughed away
On Lea's fair banks the idle day,*
Whose love would ne'er my breast allow
To hold concealed the thoughts that now
    Within my heart are pent
Who hung upon my every breath,
Of those dear friends I mourn the death
    Of forty-five per cent.
And Harry Gray, my soul's delight,
The brave, the eloquent, the bright,
    The versatile, the shifty,
Stretched hopeless on his dying bed,
With failing strength and aching head,
In cholera's malignant phase,—
Ah! woe is me,—will shortly raise
    The average to fifty.

*The former East Indian College of Haileybury stood within a mile of the river Lea.

And when, before the rains in June,
The mercury went up at noon,
To nine-and-ninety in the shade,
I every hour grew more afraid
    That doctor Fayrer right is
In hinding to my wife that those
Inflammatory symptoms rose
    From latent Hepatitis.
I'll, ere another week goes by,
For my certificate apply,
    And sail home invalided:
Since, if I press an early bier,
The deaths from Liver in the year,
Compared with those produced by Sun,
Will (fearful thought!) have then by one
    Their ratio exceeded.

The traditional Independence Day poem is a thing of the past. But once citizens across the land gathered on that historic day to hear poets laboriously declaim on the topic of independence. The motives may have been exalted, but the poetry usually wasn't.

The following, declaimed in San Francisco on July 4, 1886, commits such atrocities as rhyming *George* with *charge*, reversing name order, mixing words such as *oriflam(b)* with words such as *shebang,* and suggesting that young children grow up to become nation-states. Today's alternative to the Independence Day declamation—watching a parade on TV with a bag of potato chips—seems preferable.

Independence Day

In days of old, certain patriots bold,
    When England grew pedantic,
Unfurled to the gale the Mayflower's sail
    And ferried o'er the Atlantic.

On Plymouth rock was landed the stock
    With modest oriflamb
Who framed the state we perpetuate,
    Entitled our *Uncle Sam*.

The infant grew, as infants do,
    Into a youthful nation;
When the English yoke began to choke
    And it cried for emancipation.

Then England thought, as England ought,
    We're losing by relaxation;
We'll keep them down by oppression's frown
    And the grinding heel—*taxation*.

. . .

Those patriots old, so we are told,
    Didn't like *tax* on their tea;
So they threw it away in Boston Bay,
    For the mermaids down in the sea.

Then John Bull came across the main
    To stop this Yankee row. . . .
But Washington George, the man in charge,
    Before he began to strike,

Held up his saber and said, "Kind neighbor,
   Whichever end you like."

. . .

So one hot July day John Hancock did say,
   To a large continental audience;
I've a Yankee notion to make a motion
   For Declaration of Independence.

. . .

When, in human events, with good intents,
   Two nations are tired of sticking;
If one has the grit to make the split,
   There's no use in the other's kicking.

We may be the scion of the "British Lion"
   But listen to my harangue:—
The American *crow* will let 'em know
   We can run our own *shebang*.

. . .

That great Declaration made by the nation
   Tells the reason why,
With great demonstration and more perspiration,
   We celebrate Fourth of July.

❧ The Worst Poem Ever Written ❧
in the English Language

It is no easy task to designate one very bad poem as the absolute epitome of awfulness. But in going through hundreds of selections, one poem stood out —"A Tragedy"—which, indeed, it was. Our opinion was shared by the Not Terribly Good Club of Great Britain, an organization dedicated to following and celebrating failure, as well as by a motley assortment of friends, writers, and critics.

The poet who inflicted this work on the world was Theophile Marzials, a poet/librarian with a flair for the melodramatic. Born in Belgium in 1850, educated in Switzerland, and finding employment in England, Marzials had long blond hair, a baritone voice, and a continental-sized ego. He once interrupted a hushed library room by loudly declaiming: "Am I not the darling of the British Museum Reading Room?" He also had an enthusiastic propensity for giving impromptu public recitals of his works. The reaction of the public can only be guessed at.

A Tragedy

by *Theophile Marzials*

Death!
Plop.
The barges down in the river flop.
Flop, plop,
Above, beneath.
From the slimy branches the grey drips drop. . . .
To the oozy waters, that lounge and flop. . . .
And my head shrieks—"Stop"
And my heart shrieks—"Die.". . .

Ugh! yet I knew—I knew
If a woman is false can a friend be true?
It was only a lie from beginning to end—
My Devil—My "Friend.". . .

So what do I care,
And my head is empty as air—
I can do,
I can darc
(Plop, plop
The barges flop
Drip, drop.)
I can dare, I can dare!
And let myself all run away with my head
And stop.
Drop
Dead.
Plop, flop.

Plop.

Acknowledgments

First, very heartfelt thanks to our editor, Marty Asher, who believed, as we do, that very bad poetry is in its own muddy way somehow sublime, who was filled with great suggestions, and who even laughed at our jokes.

Thanks, of course, to our always optimistic agent Kris Dahl for not giving up on our idea; to Kim Kanner for being always wonderful and Minsun Pak for being ever helpful; to Katy Barrett and Anne Messitte for having such great ideas; and to Margaret Harris, Andre Barcinski, Angela Vitale, Paul Kroehnke, Jonathan Brecht, Ed Kenna, Stratton Leopold, and Susan Dumois for all their help. And to Mitch Callanan and Sylvia and Alex Petras for listening to us recite bad poetry over and over and over. . . .

We would also like to thank the very *good* poets who were so kind to us: John Hollander, Donald Justice, Galway Kinnell, and Richard Wilbur. Special thanks to Sandra McPherson and Charles Wright for bravely daring to share with us examples of their own worst verse—which, unfortunately, was, in spite of their own assessment, much too good to be included in this collection. And extra-special thanks to W. D. Snodgrass, who shares our love of lamentable verse and contributed several gems to this collection.

About the Editors

Kathryn and Ross Petras are a brother and sister who fondly recall laughing at each other's early poetic efforts, most notably Ross's "Pinky Bee," which even by first-grade standards was lamentable, and Kathy's adolescent "Man-Smell," which is fortunately lost. Nevertheless, Kathy went on to win several awards for her poetry in college; while Ross won commendations for writing non-poetic bureaucratese for the U.S. Department of State. Both now enjoy writing books for a living, which include *World Access,* a compendium of world culture, and *The 776 Stupidest Things Ever Said,* a best-selling collection of verbal foolishness.